THE DAILY JOKER

To Charley,

Chortle Charley!

GARETH P. JONES AND RACHEL DELAHAYE

Piccadilly
PRESS

First published in Great Britain in 2018 by
PICCADILLY PRESS
80–81 Wimpole St, London W1G 9RE
www.piccadillypress.co.uk
Text copyright © Gareth P. Jones, Rachel Delahaye, 2018
Illustration copyright © Nigel Parkinson, 2018
A CIP catalogue record for this book is available from the British Library.
ISBN: 978-1-84812-789-0
also available as an ebook

1
Printed and bound in Great Britain by Clays Ltd, Elcograf S.p.A.

Piccadilly Press is an imprint of Bonnier Zaffre Ltd
www.bonnierbooks.co.uk

To my mum, who has a weakness for terrible puns and has never eaten a mushroom without making a joke about not having 'mush-room' for anything else.
G. P. J.

To my mum, who makes me laugh (and always in a good way).
R. D.

THE DAILY JOKER

A Belly-Wobbling Joke for Every Day of the Year

Welcome to *The Daily Joker*! This is a joke book with a difference because you hold in your hands a guarantee that you will laugh all year round.

More than that, this book will actually teach you how to be funny! If you think you are already funny, we'll help you become EVEN FUNNIER. If you don't think you are funny, this book will prove you wrong.

We promise to provide you with a high-calibre joke to tell every single day, and a weekly joke challenge to help you develop your comedic skills.

We'll answer such questions as: why did the chicken cross the road? Who is knock-knocking at the door? When is a door not a door? And, why don't cannibals eat clowns?

By the end of the year, you'll have learned how to write and tell jokes, how to make pithy comments and how to have your audience in stitches. No comedy stone will remain unturned.

All we ask in return is a pledge that you promise to find the funny side of life, and laugh, no matter what. If you think you are up to this challenge, please place your hands on your funny bones (that's one on each elbow) and read this JOKER'S PLEDGE in a loud, clear voice in front of at least one witness.

With hand on heart I promise to try
Each day of every year
To make the people around me laugh
And grin from ear to ear.

With hand on heart I promise to make
Them giggle and guffaw,
Chuckle and snort and hoot and howl
'Til they're rolling on the floor.

With hand on heart I promise I will
Do my very funny best.
And until I've laughed my guts up
I shall never, ever rest.

Please keep *The Daily Joker* somewhere safe. Maybe you can keep it on a shelf. That would make it a shelf-help book. Or in a sock drawer, since you'll be laughing yours off. Or inside your pillow. You know, just *in case*.

Wherever you keep it, you'll need to open it every day to read your daily joke. Maybe you're a morning person, in which case you can read it first thing. Or maybe you want to save it for the end of the day.

But we guarantee that if you read one joke a day and complete one challenge a week, this will be your FUNNIEST YEAR EVER!

JANUARY

January is a funny old month. Last Christmas is done and dusted. Next Christmas is a million years away. It's cold, the mornings are dark, and school is looming like a big looming thing with classrooms. Maybe you have a New Year's resolution, such as giving up chocolate, sweets . . . or weeing in the bath. Maybe you've promised to eat more broccoli or be nicer to your sister. Whatever you've promised, you now have a new New Year's resolution: to be funny! So don't forget to share these daily jokes with your friends, family . . . anyone who will listen.

1st January

What do you get if you kneel on a Mars Bar?

Chocolate brown-knees.

2nd January

Why was the robot so grumpy?

He woke up too oily.

This should get me all squeaky clean. And the rust is history.

3rd January

Why shouldn't you think about
what you had for breakfast
when you're on a rollercoaster?
**Look, just trust me.
It's best not to bring it up.**

4th January

It's **World Braille Day**. Braille had a *bumpy*
beginning. It started off as a way for soldiers
to communicate in the dark but then Louis
Braille (who was blind himself) got hold of it
and developed it. Apparently, he had a *feeling*
it would work.

So here's your Braille joke.

Have you heard about this new kind of
car, which can be safely driven by blind
people and operated using Braille?
**At the moment it's still a bit touch
and go.**

5th January

Why doesn't Doctor Who like jam?
**Because it's jam,
and *Who* doesn't like jam!**

6th January

Why did the tailors fall in love?
Because they were so well suited.

7th January

How do you threaten a diary?
Say its days are numbered.

Joke Challenge:
Phrase One

Today's joke plays with the double meaning of the phrase 'your days are numbered'. Your challenge is to make up your own joke using a phrase that has another meaning – or one that can be twisted to mean something else. How about one of these?

'It's not rocket science' (rocket is also a kind of salad leaf)

'Pull yourself together' (try taking that literally)

'That'll cost an arm and leg' (as Frankenstein said when asked to make a monster).

If you're struggling to think of a phrase, ask someone you know, or just listen until someone uses one in everyday conversation.

> **Comedy Tip** Try to avoid using any words from the phrase in the set-up line. That way the punchline will come as a bigger surprise - so will be funnier.

Write your phrase joke here:

....
....
....
....
....

8th January

What's a dentist's favourite dance?
Flossing.

9th January

Why do hairdressers often fall out?
Because they're so snippy.

10th January

How does a skunk know it's a skunk?
'I stink therefore I am.'

11th January

Why should you never argue in a lift?
Because things can escalate quickly.

12th January

I can never take the letters 'u' & 'n' very seriously.
I mean, they're just a bit of fun really, aren't they?

13th January

It's the birthday of **Paddington creator, Michael Bond,** today, which is a fine excuse for a couple of unBEARable jokes. So grab yourself a drink of

Koka-koala and a blue-bear-y muffin and wait for the joke of the day. It's coming . . . Any minute now . . . Bear with me (as Mr Brown said to Mrs Brown when he found Paddington) . . . Ready, teddy, go!

Why doesn't Paddington wear shoes?
Because of his bear feet.

14th January

Did you hear about the puppet master who went crazy?
He started throwing Punches.

Joke Challenge:
Talk to the Hand

Today's joke is a reference to Punch and Judy, and puppets can be a great source of humour. Maybe you have a favourite hand puppet and you fancy trying your hand at ventriloquism (you make it look as if the puppet is doing all the talking while you sit there as tight-lipped as you can!).

All you need is a puppet (a sock will do), a couple of jokes and a bit of practice.

Comedy Tip It's always funny when you get into an argument with your puppet. Have your puppet be cheeky. Practise in a mirror and try mastering the art of looking embarrassed or annoyed by your puppet.

What's wrong with you?

I've got lockjaw.

What's lockjaw?

I can't open gy gouth groggily.

That makes my job easier.

15th January

Why is it hard to take pictures of mythical creatures with digital cameras?

They come out pixie-lated.

Let's do an elf-y!

16th January

Why are knights' stories so boring?
They tend to dragon.

17th January

What's green and sticky and found in tissues . . . ?
Snot what you think.

18th January

It's **A. A. Milne's birthday**. He wrote the Winnie-the-Pooh stories, which he based on his son's toy. The stories became so popular that nowadays everyone loves Pooh. There are cuddly Poohs, televisions programmes about Pooh and people even go to the cinema just to get a look at an extra-large size Pooh. If you think that's funny, then you are definitely someone who likes toilet humour. But let's wipe that thought from your mind as we get on with today's Pooh jokes.

Of Winnie-the-Pooh's friends, I like the donkey the best.
He's totally Eeyore-some.

Why was Christopher Robin?
Because Pooh needed the honey.

19th January

Did you hear about the lorry driver and the witch?

**He turned into a road.
She turned him back.**

20th January

What do head lice watch on TV?
Nit-flix.

This show is louse-y.

21st January

I didn't completely lose my voice at the petting zoo . . .
But I did feel a little hoarse.

Joke Challenge:
Beast Jest

Write a list of animals. Put down as many as you can think of. Ask family and friends to help add to your list. Now look at which ones have more than one meaning. You'll find that lots of them are also verbs. So *badger* also means to bother. To *fox* someone is to baffle them. To *rabbit on* means to talk a lot. There are LOADS more. See how many you can find, then have a go at using one of these double meanings to make your own joke. Or think of something an animal does and use that in your punchline. Cows go moo, cats go meow and dogs go to the toilet against trees . . . Have fun with it.

Write your ANIMAL joke here:

....

....

....

....

....

....

....

22nd January

Did you hear about the royal sheep that went mad and thought he was a dog?

He was Baa King.

23rd January

Did you hear about the new laser bread knife?

It's cutting-edge technology.

24th January

Why do circus clowns have baggy trousers and large shoes?

To go with their big tops.

25th January

What's the scariest shape?
A vicious circle.

Grrrr!

26th January

It's **Australia Day**! So g'day to all our Aussie
jesters down under. We all know what you get
if you cross a kangaroo with a sheep (a *woolly
jumper*, obviously) or a kangaroo with an elephant
(*holes all over Australia*) but what if you put a
sloth on the barbie? You get a *slow cooker*. The
problem is that it takes ages and you end up with
a long *barbie-queue*. You're probably better off
using a bird. Maybe *cook-a-burra*? Mind you, you'd
have to catch it first. Remember that a bird in the
hand is worth two in the *bush*. Now, for our Aussie
joke of the day:

What do you get if you liquefy a
kangaroo?
A mar-soup-ial.

27th January

Today we celebrate the birthdays of Wolfgang
Amadeus Mozart and Lewis Carroll. Mozart
reached new heights of musical excellence, while
Carroll plumbed new depths of rabbit holes. But
they did have one thing in common – they were
a little mad in the middle. The Mad Hatter and
A-mad-eus. Now, there's an opera I'd watch.

Or listen to, if a bunch of Lewis Carroll singers
came to the door. Here are your jokes:

Why did Alice and Mozart enjoy nightlife?
**Alice liked a little drink and Mozart
knew all the bars.**

What's happened to Mozart now?
He's de-composed.

28th January

Today, some kids in my class were firing
rubber bands. They stopped as soon the
teacher arrived.
They couldn't stand detention.

Joke Challenge:
Tickle a Teacher

We don't mean *actually* tickle your teacher.
We mean make your teacher laugh. But timing
is everything with comedy, so pick your moment

carefully. Do not try this during the register or when you're supposed to be listening. Or when your teacher is at home, about to tuck into a bowl of soup. But, if you get the timing right, the ability to make your teacher laugh can be a useful skill. You could use today's joke or another that you think will tickle your teacher. Good luck.

How much did your teacher laugh?

☐ Loads.

☐ A bit.

☐ Not much.

☐ I got given extra homework.

29th January

How did Long John Silver know that his leg was being cut off?
He felt a little saw.

30th January

Did you know that it's **World Croissant Day**? Ah yes, the humble croissant . . . France's contribution to the world of breakfast food. These days, these French pastries can be found in most supermarkets but, personally, I find them useful for getting to the other side of the road. Yes, I always use a pedestrian *croissant*. Anyway, here is your croissant joke of the day:

What did the doctor say to the poorly little croissant?
You got yourself in a jam, but you'll be feeling butter soon.

31st January

It's OK to separate rabbits.
But it's not OK to split hares.

FEBRUARY

When the months of year play basketball, February never makes the team. It's just too short - twenty-eight days to be exact. But every four years, February gets given another day completely free and tries to get back on the team, claiming that it is a day taller. Surprisingly, this extra day makes a huge difference, and February does get to play - bouncing and jumping around the court like a demented frog. For this reason, every four years is called a LEAP YEAR.

1st February

Why are cats good at computer games?
They start off with nine lives.

2nd February

For my last birthday my parents hired
this guy who BLEW UP a giraffe!
Then he BLEW UP a dog! Then he
BLEW UP a parrot!

OK, so he was a balloon sculptor.

3rd February

Why do dog walkers always wear boots?

In case they step in a poodle.

4th February

I went to have a haircut the other day. **I might go and get another one cut tomorrow.**

Joke Challenge: **Time to Get Hair-larious!**

Hairdressing – it's the stuff of dreams for a joker. Not only are there plenty of words for hair, such as fuzz, tuft, lock and strand, but there are also plenty of ways to style it. Cut, chop, trim, snip, brush (we're listing some of them to *shave* you time). Lots of these words have double meanings or fit well into well-known sayings, such as 'cut to the chase' or 'close shave' or 'a brush with danger', and hairdressing salons love to get clever when coming up with a name for their business.

For your challenge, take a look at hairdressing salons near you or online and write down some of the jokey names they've given their shops. Work out what makes them funny, and then try to make up one of your own.

Favourite hairdresser name:

. . . .

Your own made-up hairdressing
salon name:

. . . .

. . . .

. . . .

. . . .

. . . .

5th February

Mum, Mum, I think Kevin's dad is
Spider-Man!
Why would you think that?
Because he said he's a web designer.

6th February

There's a bunch of superheroes who go around keeping drinks cold.
They're called the Just-ice League.

7th February

It's **Charles Dickens' birthday!**

Charles Dickens was a very famous (and extremely funny) writer. In *A Christmas Carol* when Scrooge sees a ghost he thinks he must have food poisoning. 'There's more of gravy than of grave about you,' he says. Which is every bit as groan-worthy as some of the puns in this book. Anyway, happy birthday, Chuck, here's your joke:

What dance should you do on Charles Dickens' birthday?
The Oliver Twist!

8th February

I recently learned how to canoe.
It was oar-inspiring.

9th February

It's **Pizza Day** and we all know how Good Wenceslas liked his pizza: deep pan, crisp and even. The problem with pizza jokes is that they're often too cheesy . . . and usually take too long to deliver. Anyway, here's your slice of pizza humour.

Why is it a good idea to set up a pizza business?
You make a lot of dough.

10th February

I've got this miniature cow that I keep in my pocket. It lives off the hairs on my legs, but I think I'm going to stop it doing that.
The other day it grazed my knee.

11th February

It's **Thomas Edison's birthday!** He was an American inventor who invented lots of machinery, including the movie camera. The first one was made of metal and wood – presumably Holly*wood*. His other big one was the light bulb. Yes, Edison really was switched on. What a bright spark! To celebrate this illuminating character, here's some light humour:

How do you grow a lamp?
You plant a light bulb.

Joke Challenge: **Light Entertainment**

This week's challenge is to come up with another joke on the subject of one of Edison's inventions. You could do another one about light bulbs. If you're not allowed to switch on the lights in your house, that's really *not on at all*. It's not like you aren't *bright* enough. The switch is *dimmer*. Or you could do something about the world of the movies (a world of stars, A-listers, blockbuster films, directors, actors and animation). There are lots of words connected with both things so do a little research then get writing!

Write your joke here:

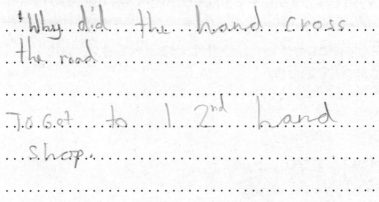

Why did the hand cross the road

To Get to l 2ⁿᵈ hand shop.

12th February

On this day in 1809 Charles Darwin was born. Darwin travelled the world on a beagle – no, wait, he travelled the world on his *ship* called the *Beagle*. Good job. He'd never have got so far had he needed to doggy-paddle all the way. Darwin discovered the answer to the question: where did we come from? I once asked my mum where she came from and she said the supermarket and could I help her in with the shopping. But Darwin discovered that we were all once single-celled creatures called amoeba just drifting about, engulfing food with nothing more than a clumsy foot and a waste hole. Maybe you know someone who's still like that.

I told my brother he was descended from a monkey.

He proved me right when he went totally ape.

13th February

If you're starting a band, why is it good to invite a chicken?

They've already got their own drumsticks.

14th February

It's **Valentine's Day**! Of course, when it comes to true love, it's best not to rush in. Avoid tennis players, for example. Love means nothing to them. And remember that true love is like good Wi-Fi – it's best when there's a strong connection. The Valentine's tradition is, of course, the 'Roses are Red' poem. They can be a bit sickly sweet –

all that love and perfume and petals. So here's an alternative one. Feel free to use it, especially good if your Valentine has a sense of humour.

Roses are red
Violets are red
Daffodils are red
Hold on, are these tinted glasses?

15th February

What do you get when there's too much greenhouse gas in your garden?
Global worming.

Think I'm going to wriggle out of work today...

16th February

Why is 'Baa Baa Black Sheep' the shortest song?

It's only got two bars.

17th February

How did the cardboard box feel about being trodden on?

It was pretty bent out of shape about it.

18th February

Why was Caesar so restless?

Everywhere he went he was always Roman.

Joke Challenge:
Lunchbox Laughter

Lunchboxes are funny. They are. Your challenge is to find something funny about your lunchbox (or a friend's) and make a friend laugh. Start off with a chatty line, such as, 'What do you think of my lunch?' and then follow it up with a joke – it can be based on a food with a double meaning, such as: 'My dog thinks it's a rabbit – it chases carrot sticks', or just a fun or silly comment, like 'My lunchbox is forming a hip-hop band – it must be all the wrappers in it.'

How did it go?

☐ They thought my humour lacked taste.

☐ They smiled but they didn't want to laugh with their mouths full.

☐ They giggled into their lunchbox.

☐ They laughed so much, food came out of their nose.

19th February

What's the difference between a
toothbrush and a toilet brush?
I don't know.
Then I'm definitely never lending you my
toothbrush.

20th February

Why are dogs so bad at telling stories?
They tend to tail off at the end.

This is such
a shaggy-dog
story.

21st February

I wouldn't call snails slow . . .
But they are definitely sluggish.

22nd February

I went to a waterpark the other day.
A dolphin did a wee on one of the
other animals.
He did it on porpoise.

23rd February

Why did the first little pig burst into
tears when his house came down?
It was the final straw.

24th February

I don't like your curtains or your wallpaper. Also, your front door is hard to open in the winter . . . Just a few home truths for you.

> **I don't get it!** A 'home truth' is a personal opinion that you might not want to hear. This joke is literally telling you home truths – opinions about your home!

25th February

Have you heard the song about the Russian prince who needed a wee?

'Tinkle, Tinkle, Little Tsar'.

Joke Challenge:
FUNursery Rhymes

Nursery rhymes have lots of joke potential. What about the parrot who wanted a nice cuppa? You know the one – 'Polly Put the Kettle On'! To create your own nursery rhyme jokes, all you need to do is look out for words that rhyme or have double meanings. To make your challenge easier we're going to give you the title of a nursery rhyme and a couple of clues and the rest is up to you.

Your nursery rhyme is **Hot Cross Buns**!
Here are your clues:

Cross can mean angry or an 'X' shape.

Buns can mean cakes, rabbits or even bottoms!

Cross rhymes with *moss, floss, boss*.

Buns rhymes with *guns, nuns, suns*.

Your best joke:

. . . .

. . . .

. . . .

. . . .

. . . .

. . . .

. . . .

. . . .

26th February

My first case was about a stolen walnut.
I cracked it.
It was a nutcase.

27th February

I didn't take the job as a
harp tuner in the end.
**There were just too
many strings attached.**

28th February

I've made a kind of indoor
shoe but every
time I put it
on I fall over.
**It's a bit
slipper-y.**

There must
have been a
slip-up in the
design . . .

MARCH

Ask any expert and they will tell you that March was named after the Roman god of Mars: god of war and chocolate. But really March was given its name because of a king who once declared that the whole country would spend an entire month marching up and down. Everyone had their *marching orders*, but when it came to it, the march descended into a massive game of 'it'. The king immediately declared his throne home-y and waited until the game was over. By then everyone was looking very tired and ruffled. It is from this that we derive the expression, Mad March Hair.

1st March

Did you hear about the bedbugs that fell in love?

They got married in the spring.

> **I don't get it!** It's common for couples to marry in springtime. These bedbugs have chosen to get married in the spring too – the mattress spring!

2nd March

Why are cats good at beating eggs?
Because they have great whiskers.

What are you making?

Cat flap-jacks.

3rd March

It's **World Wildlife Day** – a day to appreciate everything that wriggles, crawls, walks and flies. That means getting out there and walking in nature. Although of course it's hard not to walk all over nature while you're appreciating the great outdoors. Sadly, there's no *anty*-dote for a poor squashed insect, frogs don't get re-*spawned*, and a *shell*-shocked snail won't recover, so be careful where you whelk – I mean walk. If you're enthusiastic and get out there first thing in the morning, you might be treated to a view of the early bird getting the worm. Sorry, worm. No one said wildlife was always nice.

What do you say to an angry bird-watcher?

Keep your heron.

4th March

Did you hear about my new mouse soap?

It gets me squeaky clean.

5th March

I love Pancake Day.
It's just SO flipping brilliant.

6th March

Did you know elephants are good swimmers?
Is it because they're born with trunks on?
No, they swim naked.
I mean, is it because they can breath through their trunks underwater?
No, it's not that.
Then how do they learn how to swim?
They use their ears.
By flapping them?
No, they listen to their swimming instructor.
Now you're just being silly . . .

Joke Challenge:
Double Trouble

Why not try today's joke with a comedy partner? Rope someone in to work on your routine. The history of comedy is filled with double acts. Find a friend or family member to work with and see what you can come up with. You could use today's routine but it will be better if you make it your own.

> **Comedy Tip** It used to be that you had one 'straight man' and one funny one, but these days it's more common for both halves of the act to chase the laughs.

Now find an audience and perform your routine. How did it go down?

☐ We've got an agent and a booking to appear on stage at the O2.

☐ They quite liked it.

☐ They said it needed work.

☐ We've split up.

7th March

How did they catch the tinned vegetable thief?
He spilled the beans.

8th March

Today is **International Women's Day** so don't expect this joke to arrive by male. It used to be that lots of comedy was sexist and most comedians were men. Thankfully things are changing so today we celebrate our favourite female funny folk.

I've got a feeling that education for girls is very important.
Call it female in-tuition.

> **Comedy Tip** To keep your comedy funny and fair, make sure you don't use old-fashioned ideas, such as only women do washing-up and only men can be firefighters. It's not true and it's not funny.

9th March

Did you hear about the prisoner
whose escape route was blocked
by furniture?
So near, and yet sofa.

10th March

What computer console
does Hermione Granger have?
A Nintendo Wii-tch.

11th March

Where do old people post photos
on the internet?
Insta-gran.

Joke Challenge:
Techno-Titter

The world is constantly changing around us. By the time you're old you'll probably have a self-flying car. And by the time I'm young I'll have invented time travel. This week's challenge is to produce a technology joke of your own. Try to think of as many tech words as you can: websites, bloggers, vloggers, YouTubers, whatever. There are lots of words to play with. Maybe you already know a joke with the punchline 'It's called You Twit Face'. If not, see if you can work out what the rest of the joke is.

Write your technology joke here:

....

....

....

....

....

Comedy Tip If you have a school website or intranet, see if you can share your joke with your friends online.

12th March

Why did the Grand Old Duke of York struggle to march his men to the top?

It was an uphill battle.

13th March

Did you hear about the vegetarian that was invited for dinner?
He chickened out.

14th March

It's **Albert Einstein's birthday**!

Albert Einstein was an incredible mathematician and scientist who discovered new ways to measure energy, time and space. He also had funny wavy scientist hair and looked really scientist-y. He died on 18 April 1955, and, in spite of the huge contribution he made to the world of science, he only had a small funeral. In the end it was *all relatives* really. And if you don't get that joke, you really need to brush up on your Einstein.

How do you help Einstein come up with a good science equation?
Give him space and time.

15th March

Wakey-wakey! It's always around this time of year that we celebrate **World Sleep Day.** Sleep is extremely important as it gives the body and brain time to rest. There really is *safety in slumbers*! You also get to enjoy weird dreams, like the one when my pet dog was in a high chair asking for a biscuit, while my baby brother was barking and weeing against the side of a tree. At least, I think that was a dream. You might not always remember them but dreaming itself is pretty easy. You can literally do it in your sleep. Some people walk in their sleep – probably trying to find the way to the land of nod. In other snooze, here's your joke. Enjoy the rest.

Doctor, doctor, somebody put a rock in my bed!
Try not to lose sleep over it.

16th March

There were four big cats cooking. The lion was making buffalo burgers. The tiger was making deer dumplings. The puma wanted to make elk soup but the leopard was using the big saucepan to make a gazelle stew and – you know what they say – a leopard never changes his pots.

17th March

What do squirrels eat for breakfast?
Acorn flakes.

18th March

What do you get if you cover a French person in flour then put them in the oven?

Pain.

Joke Challenge:
The Write Kind of Humour

Pain means bread in French, but in English it means when something hurts. But it is not pronounced the same. In French, 'pain' is pronounced 'pan', so the joke above works on paper but not when read aloud.

Your challenge this week is to find a word that doesn't sound exactly how it's written and work a joke around it. Find a book and read a few pages, looking out for words that look like one thing on paper but sound different when spoken out loud. There are millions but here are a few to think about: *lead* (could be the metal or the past or present of to lead), *wound* (could be from 'to wind' or it could mean an injury), *sewer* (could be someone who sews, or a place where waste goes), *row* (as in what you do in a boat or when you argue).

Write your joke here:

....

....

....

....

....

....

....

....

19th March

How did the imaginary friend feel when his imaginary friend bought him an imaginary present?

He was totally made up.

20th March

Cheer up, it's **International Day of Happiness**.
Being happy is a state we all want to go to, but
you can't catch a bus to your happy place. You
have to find it within yourself, which means you
don't need to pay a bus fare. Some people find
joy hanging around animals – happy bunnies,
happy pigs in muck, happy larks, happy clams.
Some say laughter is the best medicine but,

in most cases, medicine is more effective. Otherwise, doctors would all be comedians, while stand-up comedians would have more patients. So stay happy and enjoy today's happy joke.

What do young peas sing at birthday parties?

If you're a pea and you know it, clap your hands.

21st March

It's **World Poetry Day.** Did you know, poets don't usually watch television (it depends what sonnet) – they prefer to read dictionaries (they know what a Wordsworth). But when all's said and Donne, what a poet really loves is meaning. You can't say there's no rhyme or reason to a good poem! From Michael Rosen to John Milton, Pam Ayres to Spike Milligan, there's a poet for everyone. And if you're still not convinced, go take a haiku!

Here's our joke poem for today:

A man who was after great fame

Thought poetry might make him a name.

He spent a long time

Choosing words that'd rhyme

But he forgot all about scanning and the poem was a bit lame.

22nd March

What a day. I mean, *water* day. Yes, it's **World Water Day**, and you'd have to be a total drip not to bathe in the glory of this incredible substance. Without water, there is no life. Without water, there is also no water fight – tap into some quickly, or the *soak* will be on you! Now you've got a thirst for that miracle liquid, let's raise a glass and enjoy today's pour effort.

Why did the alphabet Q to P?

Because it drank H to O.

I don't get it! When scientists talk about water they say H_2O. It means two helium atoms and one oxygen atom combine to make water. We've turned it into an alphabet joke, using Q to mean queue and P to mean pee (which is what you do when you drink too much water!).

23rd March

It's **World Meteorological Day**, which means today we forecast a weather joke. It could be *good* or it could be *poor* – it could even be *fair to middling* with a *chance of light breezes and sunny spells*. Let's face it, the joke will probably be a bit *under the weather* so feel absolutely low pressure to *laugh out cloud*. Hoping things will *brighten up later on*, here it is:

How did the sun make the snowman cry?

It gave it a thaw bottom.

24th March

Harry Houdini was born on this day in 1874. He was a famous escapologist who would do the most outrageous stunts – once he was chained up inside the belly of a whale! Did he cry? Of course not, he wasn't a blubber. Houdini often risked his life to show off his skills, like being buried alive in a box deep underground with no air to breathe. He came out coffin, of course. Fancy yourself as the new Houdini? Well, you can't escape from the joke of the day . . .

What do Superman and Houdini
have in common?
They both had an S cape.

25th March

Why are postal workers natural
comedians?
It's all in the delivery.

Joke Challenge: **The Way You Tell 'Em**

Today's joke refers to the fact that a comedian needs to have a good 'delivery'. Delivery simply means the way in which you tell your joke. Because there's definitely more than one way to do it. If you take a look at some comedy routines by stand-up comedians, you'll see how different their delivery is. Here are a few common methods:

- Get everyone's attention first, then tell your joke with confidence.

- Drop your joke into a conversation.

- Start laughing before you tell your joke, so people wonder what's funny.

- Tell your joke deadpan – with no expression.

Now choose a joke you find really funny and practise telling it. Use whichever method you think works best and deliver it to an audience.

How did it go down?

- ☐ They loved it.
- ☐ They quite liked it.
- ☐ They said it needed work.
- ☐ They told me not to give up the day job but I'm a kid and I don't even have a day job!

26th March

How do computer programmers dry their underwear?
On line.

27th March

It's **World Theatre Day,** so let's celebrate all the fine comedy actors who make us laugh. We love a good pantomime. And I know what you're thinking. *Oh no, you don't!* But, genuinely, we do. So here is today's joke:

Why did the theatre audience boo the jogger?
It was a stage he was going through.

28th March

Why should you never marry a pen?
It'll just run out on you.

He left me before the ink was dry.

29th March

One of my socks thinks it's a banana.
It's definitely an odd sock.

30th March

Vincent van Gogh was born on this day in 1853. Van Gogh was a Dutch painter who left an everlasting *impression* on us all. His paintings were *impressionist*, meaning they weren't altogether lifelike, they just gave us a sense of the subject. Speaking of senses – van Gogh famously chopped off his ear. His what? You heard. But we should remember Vincent van Gogh for the incredible pictures – *Sunflowers*, *Irises*, *Starry Night* – and for the confusion over how to pronounce his name. Some say it's van GO (USA) and others say it's van GOFF (UK) and the Dutch say van HOHK. You can say it however you want, so long as you laugh at this joke.

Why did van Gogh die poor?
He was never interested in Monet.

> **I don't get it!** Claude MONET was another impressionist painter who was working at the same time as van Gogh. The 't' in MONET is silent, so his name is actually pronounced MONAY, which is very similar to MONEY!

31st March

APRIL

April comes from the Latin word 'to open' because it's all about blooming flowers. Talking of which, what do you call a shocking bunch of flowers? A BOO-quet. That's a silly joke but flowers are all so childish in spring. They really do need to *grow up*. April also contains St George's Day. He's most famous for convincing the world that he beat a non-existent creature, which is quite some feat . . . presumably dragon feet. Maybe there was some kind of clause that meant he wasn't allowed to talk about it. You know, dragon claws.

1st April

Did you know that in the fourth month of a year, all cars use lemonade instead of petrol?

Really?
APRIL FUELS!

Joke Challenge: April Fools

Yes, you've got until midday to do as many April fools tricks as possible. Although some people play rotten tricks like throwing custard pies, it's actually much cooler if you get tricksy with some words instead. April Fools is all about toying with gullibility – that's when you blatantly tell a lie so brilliantly that others believe you. If you can do it with a little jokery to boot, you'll get double laughs. Because you'll be laughing at your gullible friend and they'll be laughing at your stupendously excellent joke. If you're having problems coming up with an idea, there's this hat you can buy on Amazon that makes your brain work faster. True. Get your thinking cap on . . .

And when you've got up off the floor after falling for that one, make up your own. Write it down as a little memento of your victory!

2nd April

It's **Hans Christian Andersen's birthday.** Hans was famous for writing loads of classic fairy tales, such as *The Little Mermaid*, *The Ugly Duckling* and *The Snow Queen*. But did you know that his sister had a daughter who was very clumsy and often fell into the flower beds?

Still to this day, you'll hear people say
'Hans' niece, Ann, bumps a daisy.'

What happened to the Ugly Duckling
in the end?
He swanned off.

3rd April

What do currants say first thing in the
morning?
**Grapey, grapey! It's time to raisin
shine!**

4th April

It's **International Carrot Day** but I'm not going to
rabbit on about that – you'll only get twitchy and
I'm worried you might be a thumper. Unless your
name is Warren, in which case you probably feel
completely at home with rabbit jokes. But let's
not hop off topic. Because this is about carrots,
and this is a day we let that long, orange beautiful
root shine. Here's a 24-carrot gold joke:

What martial arts do rabbits use to defend themselves?

Carrot-e.

5th April

What's a motor thief's favourite colour?

Khaki.

6th April

There are things I like and don't like about the playground.
It's all swings and roundabouts really.

7th April

It's **International Pillow Fight Day,** where people all over the planet *THWACK!* each other with pillows. It may feel like soft punches but things can heat up quickly. Be prepared by always fighting with a pillow in each hand – one to whack and the other to cushion the blows. My brother says he's got proof that I hit him in the face with a pillow and he's not going to take it lying down. I'm worried he's got a case . . . a pillowcase. And if you don't think that's funny, maybe you should sleep on it.

What do you call the winner of a pillow fight?
A featherweight champion.

8th April

Why was the fish so unhappy?
**Because the crab was shellfish.
(Of course, it would never admit that.
It side-stepped the issue.)**

Joke Challenge:
Make Some Fin up!

Write your own fish joke. Make a list of all the fishy things you can think of – cod, hake, fish fingers, shrimps, whales, fins, gills, sole – then try to see if any of them have other meanings (for example, 'whales' the animals sounds the same as 'Wales' the country. Shrimp means both the animal and 'small'.) Now try to make up a joke where you use this wordplay. Here's another one we wrote:

How do fish travel on land?
On *skateboards.*

But there are plenty more fish jokes in the sea so throw your net wide and haul some in.

Write your fishy joke here:

. . . .

. . . .

. . . .

. . . .

. . . .

. . . .

9th April

I got a pop-up notification at breakfast.
What for?
To say my toast was ready.

10th April

How do you spell 'nothing'?
Don't pay any attention at school.

11th April

What do you call a bug with a sense of humour?
Ridicu-louse.

12th April

Why is 'abracadabra' for advanced magicians only?
It's difficult to spell.

13th April

What did the Lego thief say when the Lego policeman caught hold of him after he stole the Lego crown jewels?

'Lego! Lego!'

14th April

Where do businesspeople keep their pants?

In briefcases.

15th April

Did you hear about the man with the extraordinary bottom?

He became the butt of jokes.

Joke Challenge:
Tell a Big Bum Joke

There are some things that just make us laugh –
like burps and farts and bottoms. You can't
go around shouting these words, though, or
people will think you're a stinker. But if you tell
a joke, you can get away with nearly anything!
It doesn't even matter if your joke is pants or
your punchline has more cracks than a row of
bottoms, because the surprise of saying one of
those giggly words will make your audience laugh
anyhow. Why don't you try? First, take the word
you want to say. Let's look at bottoms (tee-hee);
everything has a bottom – a bag, a garden, a
barrel – so work around that.

Why did the ocean itch?
It had a sandy bottom.

Try your own bottom joke here:

....

....

....

....

....

....

....

How did it go down?

☐ It was a top bottom joke.

☐ It was a pert bottom joke.

☐ It was a soggy bottom joke.

☐ Oh bum! No one laughed.

16th April

Every time I find evidence of spiders in my house, I write about it online.

It's a website.

17th April

What do you call a sheep with one leg shorter than the others?

Lean lamb.

> **I don't get it!** Butchers sometimes sell 'lean' meat, which means the fatty bits have been removed. But LEAN also means tilting, which is exactly what a lamb would do if it had one leg shorter than the others!

18th April

Most herbs can keep secrets . . .
But thyme will tell.

19th April

How many tickles does it take to tickle an octopus?

Ten tickles.

> **I don't get it!** Say the answer not as two words, but as one . . . Get it now? Tentacles!

Joke Challenge:
Something Borrowed

We included this joke after a friend suggested it. It tickled us (actually, it ten-tickled us). So now your challenge is to go and do the same. Ask your friends, a teacher or a friendly traffic warden if they have a joke up their sleeve. Jokes are supposed to be shared, so once you have got your new joke you'll have to share one of yours too.

Write your borrowed joke here:

....

....

....

....

....

....

....

....

20th April

What do criminals like to do most on holiday?
Lilo.

21st April

How do you make an egg-lover happy?
Crack a good yolk.

22nd April

It's **Earth Day**. And I don't know about you, but I'm a big fan of this planet. It's just got such a great atmosphere. If you're committed to looking after our planet, then ride the road ahead using the *recycle* path and go green. (Honestly, the alien look is SO HOT right now.) Me, I like my planet like I like my jokes: clean.

What does the Earth eat every morning?
A continental breakfast.

Joke Challenge:
Something Funny in the Air

People have been denying climate change for a while – and it's definitely a subject that's been heating up. They say comedy gets the message across, so why not joke about it! This time, generate an observational joke. Use a set-up line, such as: *The earth's warming up so much* . . . and then add a jokey observation line such as . . . *I just saw a chicken lay an omelette*. Think about what other disasters might happen if everything got too hot – people shopping in their swimwear, ice cream melting the minute it's scooped, the sea boiling.

Write your best joke here:

. . . .

. . . .

. . . .

. . . .

. . . .

. . . .

23rd April

Today is thought to be the birthday of the most famous playwright ever to have written a play. **Happy birthday, William Shakespeare**! We don't know a lot about his day-to-day life but we do know why Shakespeare didn't have a cat. He just couldn't decide on *tabby or not tabby*. It was clear he was pining for a pet, however, as he wrote a play called *The Taming of the Shrew*, although we don't think he actually ever owned or tried to tame a shrew himself. His most famous comedy was *A Midsummer Night's Dream*, which featured a man with a donkey's head called Bottom. He's quite an ass. Shakespeare also died on this date but his plays live on, so happy birthday, Billy!

What was Shakespeare's favourite thing at school?
Playtime, of course.

24th April

Why should you never tell a joke to someone eating?
Because they'll only scoff.

25th April

It's **World Penguin Day** and we all know why polar bears don't eat penguins. They can't get the wrappers off! But there's something about those flat-footed, flipper-handed monochrome beasts that makes us go *aaaaaah*. Especially when they blush – which they do when they've been fishing for compliments. Did you know, a group of penguins in the water is called a raft, which is why they never sink, and a group of penguins on land is called a waddle, which just sounds weally widiculous. Penguin species include the emperor, king, rockhopper, macaroni and fairy. Snow wonder they're one of our favourites.

What does a penguin barman say to the penguin customer?
Waddle it be?

26th April

What do you do if you need to look smart in the desert?
Put on a cac-tie!

27th April

Why did the little tyre look up
to the big tyre?

Because it was a great roll model.

You can follow
me, but don't
rubber me up the
wrong the way.

28th April

What do you say to a rooster that wants
to draw?

Cockerel-doodle-do!

29th April

It's **International Dance Day**, so get down. No, we don't mean sit down. We mean *get down*. No, get back up again. This is getting ridiculous . . . What's wrong with you? What's that – you've got no sole? Oh no, that's terrible. And two left feet? It's just getting worse. Never mind, you can always do the shuffle. I think you just sit on the floor for that. Tell you what, I'll join you and we can dance cheek to cheek. Do you know, I'm a huge fan of dancing? I thought I was the only one who owned multiple dance outfits, but then I met this guy who owned two tutus, too. Extraordinary. Anyway, let's move to the beat.

Have you heard about that new show in which famous mothers compete at dancing?
It's called *Strictly Mum Dancing*.

Joke Challenge: Cha-Cha Ha-Ha

Not all comedy is spoken. Physical comedy can be just as funny, so come up with a funny dance move and give it a name that'll get a laugh. We've had crazes such as the Floss and the Whip, so introduce something new. How about the Funky Meerkat or the Starfish Flap?

Dance name:

. . . .

How many people did you get to do it?

. . . .

Draw your dance moves below:

30th April

How did Dracula treat his secretary when he turned up late for work?

He got it in the neck.

MAY

May is famous for May Day, maypoles and 'Excuse me, miss, may I go to the toilet?' May used to be called Can, but Can didn't sound as polite. 'Mayday' is also a well-recognised call from people in trouble. Although if you're in trouble you don't really want May involved, as it's probably, possibly, might be, could be, not sure but I think so, the most indecisive month. Look at the evidence – May-be the sun will shine, May-be it will rain, May-be it will, May-be it won't. Who knows?

1st May

The first Sunday in May is **World Laughter Day** and since laughter is a subject close to our hearts, here is a celebratory poem.

Some people snigger, some people whoop,

Some guffaw, some howl and spit out their soup.

Some people hoot then apologise after,

But the sound I love most is the sound of laughter.

And now today's laughter joke:

How do you measure the speed of laughter?
In giggle-hurts.

> **I don't get it!** A **gigahertz** is a unit of measurement that measures processing speed in a computer. Naturally, we thought the speed of laughter should be measured in giggle-hurts – for those jokes where you laugh so much your tummy aches!

2nd May

What happened to the writer accused of avoiding full stops?

He ended up with a really long sentence.

3rd May

Doctor, doctor, I feel like a bag!

Yes, it sounds like you might be a carrier.

> **I don't get it!** *Carrier* means 'bag', but it is also a word for someone who carries an infection or a disease.

4th May

May the Fourth be with you! Whether Star Wars is your thing or not, you can't escape film director George Lucas' creation. Or the jokes. You've probably heard the one about Darth Vader feeling Luke's presents. Or the one about eating a wookie and finding it a little Chewy. Or how Chewbacca managed to fly the *Millennium Falcon* all on his own – in other words, Hans-free. There's a whole galaxy of jokes about Star Wars, so why fight it? Start right here, Jedi.

Why did Rey know she was in trouble when she saw the flames?
Because there's no Snoke without fire.

5th May

What's a pirate's favourite letter?
RRRR!
No, actually the C be his first love.

6th May

Clowns are so dedicated to being funny.
They'll fall over themselves to make you laugh.

Joke Challenge:
Not Just a Slip of the Tongue!

Slapstick means making people laugh by being deliberately clumsy. Or to put it another way, it means falling over in a funny way. That could be hands first with bum in the air or a twirling dizzy spin with a flump at the end. The floor's the limit! This week's challenge is to work on your slapstick. But remember, it won't be funny if you actually do hurt yourself, so remember to do it safely. We're after tears of laughter not tears of pain.

How funny was your fall?

☐ They fell about laughing.

☐ They liked it.

☐ They didn't notice.

☐ I'm now in hospital with a sprained ankle. Thanks a lot, *Daily Joker*.

7th May

Sad news about the Dutchman who wore inflatable shoes . . .
He popped his clogs.

8th May

Five little pigs went to market, but which one spent a penny?

The one that went *wee-wee* all the way home.

9th May

It's **J. M. Barrie's birthday**. He wrote *Peter Pan*, the story of the boy who never grew up. It also featured Captain Hook, who lent the crocodile a hand. Peter Pan had a friend called Tinker Bell, which is *fairy 'nough*. Sometimes he turned black and white and furry and became Peter Panda. OK, so that bit isn't true. But it could be – all you have to do is believe . . . And I believe it's time for today's pan-fried gag.

When does Peter Pan appear?
Wendy window is open.

10th May

What happens if you cross a werewolf with a cow?
Something that likes to howl at the mooooon.

11th May

Why do tailors make natural comedians?
They have excellent material.

12th May

What's better than a unicorn on a scooter?
A bike horn on a bicycle.

13th May

What do you call a woman buried up to her neck on the beach?
Sandy.

Joke Challenge: Name That Joke!

There are as many joke names as there are name jokes. What do you call a man with a spade in his head? **Doug!** What do you call a man who no longer has a spade in his head? **Doug-less.** What do you call a woman tied to a boat? **Maud** (*moored*). Or you can add surnames too: what do you call a girl with a thousand legs? **Millie Pede.** What do you call a man who has just been playing reggae? **Ben Jammin.**

Your challenge is to come up with your own. Find a list of names and see what you can do to make it into the punch line.

Write your name joke here:

. . . .

. . . .

. . . .

. . . .

14th May

In the annual pirate sailing race how can you tell which team is doing badly?
The one that's flagging behind.

15th May

I'm taking a vow of silence.
For how long?
I can't say.

16th May

I just wrote a book.
Wow. How long did it take?
Not long. It's only two words.

17th May

Did you hear about the shoe who made a deal with the devil?

He sold his sole.

18th May

It's **International Museum Day**. There are all kinds of museums. There's one about cows (*moo-seum*), one about cats (*meow-seum*) and one about who-knows-what (*Natural Mystery Museum*). Full of fascinating exhibitions, museums are home to old bits of the past. Most of us are touched by the experience, though touch the displays and a museum guard will make you admit to your crime.

What's hard and cold and goes clunk in the dark?

A knight at the museum.

19th May

I know a head louse who thinks he's
Oscar Wilde.

He's such a nitwit!

I don't get it! Oscar Wilde was a WIT, meaning he was clever
and funny. A NITWIT is the opposite! It's a person who does or
says silly things. In this joke, a head louse thinks he's clever,
but he really isn't!

20th May

It's **World Bee Day** so make a *beeline* for some
sweet punny-coated gags. For example, did you
know you have to pass an exam to become a
professional beekeeper? It's a multiple-choice
quiz . . . the answers are mostly *Bs*. There's
always a bonus question or two at the end – why
do beekeepers get more honey in the summer?
Because that's when it's *swarm*ing up. And for
another bonus point – why are bee-keepers good
at television quiz shows? Because they're used to
having their fingers on *buzzers*. Well, I found that
funny . . . but then again, *hive* probably gone mad.
Let's buzz on with the next joke!

What did Dracula say to the bee?
I vant to bite your nectar.

Joke Challenge:
Create a Buzz

With all your joke-telling you should have created a buzz of excitement among your family and friends. It's time to put on a show. Start off with people you know well and perform it somewhere you're comfortable, such as your kitchen or the playground. Get together some of your favourite jokes and practise telling them – perhaps get a funny friend to join in for some variety. Once your act is ready for an audience, have a go at designing a funny poster advertising your show – you'll need to give your act a name and make the advertising as bright and exciting as possible.

21st May

I went camping with all of my family last weekend.

It was intense.

22nd May

Happy birthday, Sherlock Holmes creator, Sir Arthur Conan Doyle! He might be dead and buried now, but his fictional detective lives on. He even managed to survive being killed by his creator, which is pretty impressive. Did you know that Sherlock's sidekick Watson narrates the books? Watson learned about detective work from Sherlock. In other words, Watson was *Holmes-schooled*. To an *elementary* level, anyway. Now, do I detect a joke?

Why is Sherlock the perfect TV companion?
Because he knows Watson.

23rd May

It's **World Turtle Day**. A lot of people don't know the difference between a tortoise and a turtle. Well, a tortoise is a land-dwelling reptile, while a turtle is *turtle*y different! Turtles live in the sea, just paddling about and being nice. They have a diet of jellyfish, which means their tummies wobble. But not to worry, they are protected by a hard shell and should be treated like *shell-ebrities*.

What game do turtles play at birthday parties?
Terrapin the tail on the donkey.

24th May

It's **Queen Victoria's birthday.** By complete coincidence, she happened to reign during an era called the Victorian age. Spooky, eh? Victoria was known as a humourless queen, famous for saying, 'We are not amused.' Perhaps she was talking to a butcher and actually said 'We are not *ham*used.' Apparently, she was always very clean and well bathed. She used a *Victoria sponge*, of course. Despite her grumpy face, black clothing and reputation as a sour-faced monarch, in private she was apparently an absolute hoot with a marvellous lust for jokes. Although I'm not sure she would like this one:

Queen Victoria built Albert Bridge to commemorate her late husband.
She never really got over it.

25th May

Did you know that dinosaurs were also excellent shopkeepers?

Oh yes, they did a roaring trade.

26th May

Why did the banana push the apple off the table?

The banana had gone bad.

27th May

Do you want to hear a telepathic joke?
. . . *(pause)*
What did you think?

28th May

It's **Ian Fleming's birthday.** He created the world's most famous spy, James Bond. He did not create the world's most famous pie, which is apple pie. Bond is such a good spy that his catchphrase is saying his own name: Bond, James Bond. It's a genius disguise – but only if he's disguised as himself. Which isn't very spy-like. Fleming also created characters with marvellously interesting names, such as Miss Moneypenny, Goldfinger and Scaramanga. Makes you wonder if he was having a bad day when it came to M. But we would never criticise Fleming – it would be an absolute *Dr No-No*. Come, let's get on with the real joke, before they take away our licence to kill you with laughter . . .

When 007 marries, we'll never find out.
Why not?
It'll be a secret service.

Joke Challenge:
I Spy a Joke

Inside the world of espionage there are some truly criminal jokes. Think of all the gadgets to play with – invisible ink, poison-dart pens, amphibious cars – and the spy lingo, like 'top-secret dossier' and 'license to kill'. You can easily make up a joke about being undercover or use spy-nicknames, such as moles, rats, agents, narks and snoopers, which have multiple meanings.

Comedy Tip Make it even more authentic by using secretive language.

(Pssst, did you hear the Secret Service arrested a dog?
They picked him up for being Snoopy.)

Good luck, Agent Double Ho-Ho Seven.

29th May

What do you get if you cross a crocodile with a chest of drawers?
A snappy dresser.

30th May

Why are cowboys no good at accurately counting cows?

They tend to round them up.

31st May

I like to unwind by firing at a range of cheese.

You know, just shooting the bries.

> **I don't get it!** The term 'shooting the breeze' means sitting back and relaxing. And brie is a type of cheese.

JUNE

June contains the summer solstice, which was celebrated by the ancient druids at Stonehenge. These wizards took a number of large lumps of rock, and rolled them from Wales to Wiltshire. It is probably the most severe example of holiday overpacking in history since they were only going for the weekend. Experts believe that before thousands of years of erosion took place, the stones were carved into the shape of giant chickens, which is where it got its name. Wait for it . . . yes, it used to be called Stone Hens!

1st June

Who is the most famous June?

(Give them a moment to guess)

Nope?

June Know-who-l-am?

2nd June

What is a horse's favourite pasta?
Spaghetti bolog-*neighs*.

3rd June

It's **World Bicycle Day** so we've changed gear for today's joke. We did consider using the one about the dangerous patch of concrete that turned out to be a *cycle path*. Or the one about the bike-shop owner who started wearing bicycles, going from *peddling his wares* to *wearing his pedals*. Or the joke about the cyclist who gave up drinking because he couldn't handle bars. In the end we pumped for . . .

That woman from the International Bicycle Association . . .
She's a great spokesperson.

4th June

Did you hear about the spy who hid in a bath?

He was a bubble agent.

5th June

I've written 1, 2, 3, 4, 5, 6, 7, 8, 9 on my cornflakes.

Why?

To give them cereal numbers.

6th June

Why's the new Doctor Who such a good musician?
She's always in time.

7th June

Teacher: What's the difference between 'don't' and 'do not'?
Pupil: One means not doing something, the other has jam in the middle.

8th June

Today is **World Oceans Day**. You might know this joke: why was the beach wet? Because the seaweed. But these days the oceans and beaches have a different kind of waste problem. It's full of our rubbish, and it's killing marine life. Far from shipshape, we are quite literally making our seas sick. It's nothing to laugh about, but there's nothing wrong with telling a joke to remind us how important our seas are. So without further ado, let's *seas* the day and tell a tale to warm our cockles.

Why do fish and chip shops rarely sell sardines?
Because they're small fry.

> **I don't get it!** 'Fry' doesn't just mean heating something up in oil; it's also the word for baby fish. And if you call something 'small fry', it means it's so small it's not worth bothering with.

9th June

Waiter, waiter, there's something sticky on my sausage!
Yes, it's a sausage on a stick, sir.

I said I was so hungry I could eat a STEAK!

10th June

How do you make milkshake?

(Wait for answer. Most people you ask will give you an answer about giving a cow a pogo stick or putting a cow in a freezer. Now give your answer in your best deadpan voice . . .)

Er, no. You put ice cream and milk into a blender.

Joke Challenge:
The Anti-Joke

There are some jokes so old that they've gone well past their best-before date. Being funny relies on saying something unexpected, so if your audience knows the punchline, you can't surprise them. That's when you'll need . . . THE ANTI-JOKE! Lure them in with a classic set-up line, wait for them to say the punchline, then deliver your anti-joke with a totally straight face.

11th June

Some people sleep with their eyes open.
I just don't know how they kip awake!

12th June

Why are mountaineers never satisfied
with just one mountain?
They like to see a range.

13th June

Why do Americans wear T-shirts?
They believe they have the right to bare arms.

I don't get it! Americans believe in the right to *BEAR* ARMS, which means the right to carry weapons. *Bare arms* are what you see a lot of in summer!

14th June

Why is toast so lovely?
No idea. It's just bred that way.

15th June

What should you use if you have a pretend cold?
A tissue of lies.

16th June

Why are nudists so relaxed?
They let it all hang out.

17th June

Before getting married, my girlfriend
and I threw a big pot of crimson paint
over our heads.
Then we were wed.

Joke Challenge:
Funny Voice

Today's joke works best if you put on a funny
voice that involves pronouncing your Rs as Ws, so
say *girlfwiend, thwew* and *cwimson*. Not only does
this help the punchline, it's also a proven fact
that funny voices are funny. (That's why they're
called funny voices.) So work on your repertoire.
Once you've got one, try saying a variety of
things in that voice. Sometimes it helps to name

your voice and give it a bit of character. But remember, funny voices can be funny but if over-used they can drive people CRAZY.

Path me the thalt, pleath!

18th June

Today is **International Sushi Day** and **International Picnic Day**, so it only makes sense that you celebrate with a sushi picnic. But no, that doesn't mean it's OK to eat the family goldfish in the garden. Sushi is a Japanese cuisine that involves raw fish, whereas picnics are a British tradition that involve sore bottoms. Picnics usually require a flat patch of land, whereas it's better to eat sushi on a slope. Why?

Because sushi rolls . . . In restaurants sushi is often served on a conveyor belt. If you haven't experienced it we recommend it. It can be really quite moving.

What do you do if your friend won't come to your sushi picnic?
Invite salmon else . . .

19th June

I keep a note of every vegetable I eat.
I often think, well, there's a turnip for the books.

> **I don't get it!** A 'turn-up for the books' is an expression that means a surprise – often a good surprise. So if you were interested in vegetables, digging up a turnip would be a very good surprise. It so happens that 'turnip' sounds very much like 'turn-up'.

20th June

Sight, hearing, taste and smell probably wouldn't help if you're lost in a forest . . .
But touch wood.

21st June

Hey dude, did you know **International Surfing Day washes up around this time every year**? Surfers are just so cool – probably because they keep up with the *current* trends. They're happy, too, always *catching waves*. It's why I'm learning to surf, but it *shore* is harder than it looks – there's a lot to take *on board* and I'm struggling to keep my head above water. Still, if I keep trying, I'll hopefully get my surf-tificate and everything will be *swell*. How are the surf jokes so far? Surf far, so good! See how you like this one, and let's hope it's not a *total wipe-out*.

Never hang around with fish that ride on waves.

There's always a lot of surf-fish tension.

22nd June

I bought the best hat the other day.
It was a top hat.

23rd June

How did the moles celebrate
the field's birthday?
They gave it the bumps.

24th June

Why did the comedian purr
after every joke?
It was his cat's phrase.

Joke Challenge:
Catchphrase

Catchphrases are often-repeated sayings,
usually by famous people, fictional characters or
advertising slogans. Examples include:

'Oh crumbs!' (from the character of Penfold in
Dangermouse)

'I'm lovin' it' (famous burger restaurant slogan)

'Yes we can!' (44th US president, Barack Obama).

A catchphrase that everyone knows will work really well as a punchline to a joke. You may already know some slogans or catchphrases. This week's challenge is to work on your own catchphrase. It doesn't have to be complicated. In fact, the simpler, the better, such as, 'It's the way I tell 'em' or 'I don't believe it!' – so have fun and choose one that fits you.

Write your catchphrase here:

....

....

....

....

....

....

25th June

It's **Global Beatles Day**! Yeah yeah yeah. . . We're not talking about the minibeasts in the back garden, but the British pop sensation of the 1960s, who are unlikely to be lurking around your back garden. Band members John Lennon, Paul

McCartney, George Harrison and Ringo Starr were known as the 'fab four', and their music and fame spread all over the world. Also, their name is a pun ('beat' as in a musical beat and 'beetle' as in the insect – one of their favourite bands was called The Crickets). The chances are you have heard some of their songs and you can have lots of fun turning their song titles into silly conversations like this:

Hey Jude, I Wanna Hold Your Hand.

Let it Be

We Can Work It Out

I am the Walrus, Ob-La-Di Ob-La-Da

Help!

Here's your fab-four funny for the day:

Did you know Paul McCartney composed 'Yesterday'?
He'll probably compose today as well.

26th June

What kind of car do sheep drive?
Lamb-orghinis.

27th June

It's **International Sunglasses Day**. Sunnies (as Australians call them) date back to fourteenth-century China, when they were designed to hide emotions (so, *emotion glasses* or maybe *no-fun glasses*). These days some sunglasses are very expensive, although I think they're a *shade* overpriced. So, *lens* us your ear and allow us to *brighten* up your day with this *squint*essential silly joke.

What kind of sunglasses do donkeys wear?
Bray-bans.

28th June

Did you hear about the new computer game based on charades?
It's called Mime-craft.

29th June

What do the rabbit police always carry?
Carrot batons.

30th June

My gran can move things up and down just by looking at them.
She told me she's got a stare-lift.

JULY

At some point in this month there is a good chance that you will have to say goodbye to your teacher as your school year draws to an end. Some people decide to buy their teachers presents, like the kid who bought his teacher a gerbil to keep her car neat and tidy. It turns out he had misunderstood when his teacher said she needed a *car-pet cleaner*. In the end, the teacher didn't keep the gerbil in her car. She preferred to take the *rodent less travelled*. Anyway, don't do that. Instead, why not write your teacher a card with a few of your original jokes to remember you by? But don't forget that your teachers will miss you over the summer holidays! Unless you stop moving around so they can actually hit you.

1st July

It's **International Joke Day**! It's a total joke! You're having a laugh! But every day for you is International Joke Day. We are halfway through the year and by now joking should be like breathing for you. You should be a lean, mean joking machine, the fastest pun-slinger in town, the wittiest wit in the West. So go forth into the world and . . . make 'em laugh.

Why didn't the joke work across the continents?

It was only borderline funny.

Joke Challenge:
Joke Daze

To mark the halfway point of your FUNNIEST YEAR EVER it's time to test how far you've come. For this week's challenge you'll need:

- Another person
- A timing device
- This book
- Your wits about you

Because this week's mission is to try to break the world record for the most jokes you can tell in a minute. When this book went to print the record stood at twenty-six but maybe, with a little practice, you can beat it. Even if you don't, it should be fun (and funny) to try.

How many jokes did you tell in a minute?

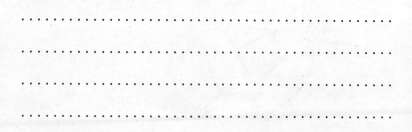

2nd July

It's **World UFO Day**. People say it's to do with aliens, but if the flying object is unidentified, *how on Earth* would they know? Quite often images of UFOs turn out to be hoaxes. Like the one that was actually an Unidentified Frying Omelette (it was more yolks than hoax) or an Unidentified Flying Oblong, although people say that there are four sides to that story . . . But the most fun of all the conspiracies is that those blurry images of discs in the sky are spaceships, full of strange little people with an interest in Earth. How a bunch of geography teachers got up there, we just don't know! Anyway, here's a joke that's out of this world.

How can you tell if a troop of soldiers is actually an alien army?
If they're Martian in formation.

3rd July

Proton: Why can't you trust atoms?

Neutron: I don't know. Why can't you?

Proton: Because they make up everything.

Neutron: That's an old joke.

Proton: You should be more positive.

Atom: Right, that's it. I'm splitting.

What was up with those two?

Dunno, must have had terrible chemistry.

I don't get it! Today's joke is all about the molecules that make up our universe. If you don't get it, try it out on a teacher or parent and see if they can explain why they're funny.

4th July

American Independence Day! On this day in 1776, the USA gave Britain the old heave-ho! Since then, it has become one of the world's most significant superpowers. It's also the birthplace of some mighty comics, like Superman, who actually did have superpowers . . . and Batman, whose superpowers are having an eye for awesome car design. America is also responsible for some of the funniest people in the world. So today we doff our cowboy hats to you and offer this super joke:

What did Captain America say when he bought flat-pack furniture?
Avengers, assemble!

5th July

I have a special holder for my pen refills.
Just ink case.

6th July

Many happy returns to the Dalai Lama, born (or possibly reborn) this day in 1935. The Dalai Lama is a Buddhist spiritualist leader, a man so calm and happy that nothing rattles his cage. He's not actually in a cage, that's just a saying – and even if he was, you can't keep a free spirit. He isn't a llama either, in case you were wondering. He overcomes fear, hatred and jealousy. He can even overcome toothache – he practises *transcend dental medication*. And that might be an old joke but at least it's in a new incarnation. Here are a couple of new ones.

Why was the Dalai Lama shelling all the beans?
To reach his inner peas.

Why does the Dalai Lama make people jump?
Because he's a BOO!-dist.

7th July

Today is **World Chocolate Day** so it's time to wave your *Snickers* in the air and yell choco-lujah! Some chocolate bars lend themselves more easily to jokes than others. With names like *Mars*,

Milky Way and *Galaxy*, you can imagine aliens thinking corner shops are signposting the way home (some even contain flying saucers). A Lion Bar can't be trusted. Why? Well, it is a *lyin'* bar. My sister always says she's going to share her chocolate but she never does. She's such a *Malt-teaser*. So let's wrap things up with a couple of choco-licious chortlers.

What kind of chocolate bar would you like?

Wispa please.

(Whisper) What kind of chocolate bar would you like?

They've invented a new type of underwear made from lots of little chocolates.

They're called Smartie-pants.

8th July

What should you do if the devil asks you to sit down?

Look for deceit.

Joke Challenge:
Making a Pig's Ear

Pigs are pretty funny and there are lots of words associated with them, on and off the plate. Snort, sow, oink, trotters, squeal, bacon, ham and gammon. And so many of those words have other meanings (bringing home the bacon, hamming it up) or can fit into other words (oink-ment, squeally good). So this week's challenge is to come up with your own pig joke. But please, no porkies!

Write your pig gag here:

....

....

....

....

....

....

....

....

9th July

Spaghetti, ravioli and macaroni are in a race. Which wins?

The first to pasta post.

> **I don't get it!** Someone who is 'first past the post' is a winner. It's used in horse racing, for example. Here we're saying 'pasta post' which sounds like 'past the' if you're using a comedy Italian accent. But there's another meaning – perhaps the post is made out of pasta too!

10th July

What did the caveman do when someone handed him two sticks?

He made light of it.

11th July

E. B. White was born on this day. He's most famous for writing *Charlotte's Web*, which is about a spider becoming friends with a pig. It was way ahead of its time really, as it was all about finding fame on the web.

Did you hear about the fastest pig in the world?

It can go from snort to sixty in under a minute.

12th July

I live next door to a factory that specialises in cheap tennis equipment.

I might move. It makes an awful racket.

13th July

It's **International Rock Day!** That doesn't mean it's an excuse for your parents to put on their favourite rock records. Today is about craggy lumps of sediment and old fossils. (Oh, maybe this is about those old rockers after all.) I once read a book called *What to Do with Stones you Find on the Beach* by Rocky Shaw. Actually, I only skimmed it. Here's your rock-solid joke:

I had a stand-up gig in a quarry the other day.
I was met with stone-y silence.

14th July

My anti-gravitational car is awful.
It drives me up the wall.

15th July

Knock knock!
Who's there?
Kanye.
Kanye who?
Kanye stop messing about and open the door!

Joke Challenge:
Knock 'Em Dead!

There are millions of *knock-knock* jokes. Some people think the first one came from Shakespeare. Presumably that was:

Knock knock!
Who's there?
Will.
William Shakespeare, the Elizabethan playwright, responsible for *Hamlet*, *Macbeth* and *A Midsummer Night's Dream*?
No, *will* you let me in or not?

They've come a long way since then, though, and now it's your time to make up a new one. Maybe you know a name that can be used as the beginning of a sentence, such as Ivor (*Ivor* key somewhere but I can't find it), Justin (*Just in* time. It's freezing out here), or Noah (*Noah* place I can stay tonight?). Good luck and please don't ring the bell. Your joke won't work as well. Brrrring your best joke!

16th July

Car wheels never get replaced.
They just get re-tired.

17th July

Smiley faces all around because it's **World Emoji Day**. These little pictures can be a great way to communicate but they'll never replace language when it comes to getting a laugh. Wordplay requires having words to play with. Show me a world without puns and I'll show you my . . . 😞

Knock knock!
Who's there?
Emoji.
Emoji who?
Emoji lawn on Thursday.

18th July

Why can you never get into a good book when you're on safari?
It's hard to read between the lions.

Can I join your book cub?

19th July

Doctor, doctor, I feel like a vampire!
That sounds a bit batty.

20th July

What do you do if you discover that your local river is polluted by tomato ketchup?
Firstly, you find the source.

21st July

What do you call a mythical creature you catch while fishing?
An into-net troll.

22nd July

What's the difference between roast beef and pea soup?
Anyone can roast beef.

Joke Challenge:
Absolute Classics

This joke is something of a classic, which shows that it's definitely worth exploring old jokes. Your parents might be a good resource for jokes that are so old that everyone has forgotten about them. So ask a parent, relative or teacher what jokes they told when they were your age.

Write your best old joke here:

....

....

....

....

....

....

23rd July

Everyone can have a slice of cake – everyone apart from criminals.
There's no piece for the wicked.

24th July

Today we say **happy birthday to Amelia Earhart**, who was the first woman to fly solo across the Atlantic Ocean. Her arms must have been very tired after that. That's silly – she was in a plane of course, all alone – apart from her pet rooster. She kept it in the *cock*pit. And it might have explained why her plane went into a *tail*spin. What a sad end to a high-flying career. Here's to you, Amelia – you were *plane* amazing.

How do you make Amelia Earhart fly?
Propel her.

25th July

What's yellow, noisy and makes a hole in the ground?
A daffodrill.

26th July

What do you call a time-travelling monkey?

Doctor Oo-oo-oo!

27th July

What sort of hat do you wear on your leg?

A kneecap.

28th July

How did Tinker Bell deliver the tragic news of Peter's demise?
Deadpan.

29th July

It's **International Tiger Day**. We should be super *fang-ful* for a day that raises awareness of these beautiful beasts. There are very few of them left in the wild – maybe they're being hunted by army sergeants, who think they're better than tigers because they've *earned their stripes*. I beg to differ. Sergeants' stripes are bits of cloth sewn on their uniform whereas tigers' stripes are *fur and away* the best! Sink your teeth into the daily joke.

What do you get if you cross a tiger with a kangaroo?
A stripy jumper.

BOING! BOING! BOING!

Joke Challenge:
Jungle Jests

There are loads of wildly funny jokes to be found lurking in jungles. Lions, tigers, elephants and leopards are all fun things to think about. Why don't panthers hunt mongoose? Because they are *mere cats*. And everyone needs to understand why there are no painkillers in the jungle. That's right, the *parrots-eat-em-all*. So now, it's up to you to hunt down a jungle joke.

Write your jungle joke here:

....

....

....

....

....

....

....

30th July

My teacher makes comments on everything I write.

Mark my words, he does.

31st July

Harry Potter turns one year older today and coincidentally it's also the birthday of someone called **J. K. Rowling**. If you plan to send Harry or his creator a birthday card, make sure you *spell* everything right and don't *wand*er off the point. When it comes to magic jokes it can be hard to know *witch* one to pick, but in honour of the world's most famous scarface, here is today's wizard joke:

What does Dumbledore say to himself when he runs out of teacups?

'A muggle do.'

AUGUST

As a word, 'August' means respected and impressive. As a month, it means NO SCHOOL! But you've still got plenty of work to do. Don't forget, you're supposed to be making people laugh all of the time – not just *summer* the time. If you find yourself stuck on a long, boring car journey, instead of asking 'Are we there yet?' look out of the window and find things to laugh at. Work out what silly things registration plates stand for or make up jokes about the names of places you pass.

Where do hairy dads come from?
Man-chest-hair!

Why do pigs avoid the Midlands?
They don't want to be anywhere near 'Burnin'ham'.

Where do you find pirates?
Crewe.

You should now be using every opportunity to put your funny where your mouth is. But one word of advice: if you find yourself on a beach this summer, don't leave your bucket and spade by the sea. You're bound to lose it. It's a *shore* thing.

1st August

What do you get if you cross a wolf and a sheep?

You'll still have the wolf but you'll need a new sheep.

2nd August

Those people who check your ticket stubs at the cinema?

You've really got to hand it to them.

3rd August

What do you get if you cross a robot with a pig?
A ham-droid.

4th August

Doctor, doctor! I feel like a pack of cards.
I'll deal with you later.
But I feel like I've only got fifty-one cards.
Then I won't be able to deal with you at all.

5th August

It's **Neil Armstrong's birthday**. He was the first man to step on the moon (Buzz Aldrin was close behind him). We earthlings celebrate this historic landing as one of humanity's greatest achievements. The race of alien moon-lice didn't see it like that and told them to 'Aldrin off'.

The astronauts never did *Apollo*-gise to the moon-lice but saying sorry is a big step for mankind. Some people think the whole moon landing was staged but then they're probably the sort of people who believe there are lice-like aliens on the moon. Sorry, I mean *lunar-ticks*!

Why did the moon go to the therapist?
It was worried about its dark side.

Joke Challenge:
Shaggy-Dog Story

The more attentive readers will have spotted that today's entry isn't entirely true. The whole thing is a load of nonsense with the 'lunar-ticks'. It's what we call a shaggy-dog story and there are a few others in this book. The trick to telling a good shaggy-dog story is to make the journey fun then throw in a surprise at the end. So either make up your own or tell a favourite joke from this book and turn it into a punchline of your own flight of fancy. Once you've got it, either write it down and show it to someone or read it out. Don't forget to make a note of how it went down.

☐ They laughed at all the right points.

☐ They laughed at the end.

☐ They shook their head and walked away halfway through.

☐ I'm still telling the story – it's somewhat longer than I was expecting.

6th August

Is it good to wear protective clothing in laboratories?

Overall, yes.

7th August

I've got a dog that's a cross between a poodle, a Great Dane, an Alsatian, a Chihuahua and a Dobermann.

What do you call it?

Jeff.

8th August

Why should you never marry a baker?

They're too needy.

9th August

What do you call a naughty old lady that likes to cause havoc?

A hooli-gran.

10th August

What's bright orange, noisy and made out of brass?

A Donald trumpet.

11th August

What kinds of toes are good to eat?
Pota-toes.

12th August

I am an avid football player.
For a while I thought I'd give
rugby a try . . .
But I couldn't convert.

Joke Challenge:
Score a Joke!

When it comes to scoring a laugh from the world
of sport, it's back of the net every time. There
are so many terms, types of equipment, rules and
sayings. I'm not very sporty but I did try my hand
at football once – I got sent off for *handball*.
I tried golf but every time I swung, the caddy
said I'd only scored '*Fore*!'. It can be expensive,

though. I had to buy a new pair of golf trousers after I got a *hole in one*. So get off the *sidelines* and *kick around* a few ideas.

Write your sport joke here:

. . . .

. . . .

. . . .

. . . .

. . . .

. . . .

. . . .

13th August

I put all my money on a horse. But it fell off when the horse moved.

14th August

What happens when wildebeest take over?
There'll be a gnu world order.

15th August

Did you hear about the fast-food employees who got engaged?

He gave her an onion ring.

16th August

Doctor, doctor! I can't see the top of your shirt.

Sounds like you're collar blind.

17th August

Music is an important part of cake making.

In what way?

I-sing!

18th August

Why did cavemen often go hungry?

Because finding food was a mammoth task.

Mmm, tough meat.

19th August

Nurse, nurse! I think I'm a cat.

OK. Well, the doctor will see you meow.

Joke Challenge:
The Doctor Will See You Now

There are lots of jokes to be made about a visit to the doctor, and the best way to think of a doctor-doctor joke is to come up with a funny complaint, such as: *Doctor, doctor! I keep thinking I'm a book –* and then have your doctor saying something like *I think you should stop telling stories* or *Now, you mention it, you do look red*. Or what about this one? *Doctor, doctor! I need you to help me out. Certainly. How did you get in?* Now, it's your turn to see the doctor but joke-writing takes time, so remember to be *patient*.

Comedy Tip Having trouble coming up with an idea? Try coming up with a punchline for this one: **Doctor, doctor! I feel like I'm invisible!** Or come up with your own animal-themed one like today's featured joke.

Write your joke here:
Doctor, doctor!

....
....
....
....
....

20th August

Why did Batman finally leave
the Batcave?

**Because Robin had been going on all
morning.**

21st August

I keep meaning to update my website
but every time I try to sit down at the
computer, my brother is on it writing his
stupid website about lumberjacks.

He's such a logger blogger PC hogger.

22nd August

Did you hear about the new superhero called Seagull Man?

He always swoops into action, when the chips are down.

He's such a super fries guy!

23rd August

How do people wash their clothes in one-storey houses?

They bung-a-load in.

> **I don't get it!** A bungalow is a one-storey house. And we talk about a 'load' of washing. We laundered the joke by combining the words! Does it wash with you?

24th August

What music do flowers listen to?

Heavy petal.

ROBERT PLANT

25th August

I sell bits of trousers.
It's a good way to make pocket money.

26th August

What does Princess Elsa say when she needs to go to the bathroom?
(sing) **Toilet it go!**

Joke Challenge: Strike the Right Note

Today's challenge involves music. Whether you like rock, pop, classical, opera, dance or jazz, there are lots of funny songs out there. You might want to find some examples first. Ask your parents if they have any favourite funny songs, then listen and see what makes them funny. After that, you'll need to write your own funny song. Don't worry if you can't play an instrument.

All you need is an idea and some funny words to rhyme. Or try writing funny words to a tune you know. Once you've written something you'll need to perform it.

How did it go?

☐ They loved it.

☐ They liked it.

☐ They thought it needed a bit of work.

☐ They threw rotten fruit at me and blocked their ears with cotton wool.

> **Comedy Tip** Listen to some of the masters of comedy songs. The music of *Flanders and Swann* might be older than your grandparents but they're definitely worth a listen.

27th August

Why was the hungry customer so cross with the Spoonerism Cafe?

It sold him a pot of lies.

> **I don't get it!** Mr Spooner was an academic who famously had a habit of swapping over the first letters of words. Named after him, a 'spoonerism' is when the initial letters of words get swapped but the sentence still makes sense. In this case the hungry customer went in for a 'lot of pies'!

28th August

My granddad is so bald that instead of a hairdo . . . he has a hair don't.

29th August

What's a cow's favourite dance?
The moooon walk.

30th August

Why did the superhero chase that guy?

Just because he spied-a-man.

31st August

Why is it easy to make Frankenstein's monster laugh?

He's already in stitches.

Lend us a hand, I've split my sides.

SEPTEMBER

It's September, which means that autumn is approaching. Americans call it *the fall* – because that's what leaves do at this time of year. Please do not read this book under a tree in the autumn. Take a *leaf* out of our book and don't catch leaves in your book. But how do leaves fall off trees in autumn? Do they just *up and leaf* or does someone pull some kind of *lever*? It must be worrying for the trees to suddenly lose all their leaves like that. Come spring, when new leaves grow, the trees must be really *re-leaved*. Or is that all too *unbe-leaf-able*. Anyway, *yew* must be *sycamore* these leaf puns so if it's *oak-a* with you, we'll make our excuses and . . . take our *leaf*.

1st September

Did you hear about the inflatable boy who took a pin to show his inflatable teacher in his inflatable school?

His teacher said, 'You've let me down, you've let the whole school down, but worst of all, you've let yourself down.'

In the end, the education system completely collapsed.

2nd September

Did you hear Ed Sheeran wrote a song about his pet sheep?

Yeah, it's called 'The Shape of Ewe'.

Joke Challenge:
Laugh at Lunch

So far we've set you challenges to make your teachers, friends and family laugh. Now it's time for the greatest challenge of all . . . make a dinner lady laugh. Maybe you know one who likes a giggle. Or maybe there's one who needs cheering up. Maybe when they're spooning sweetcorn onto your plate you can say, 'I'd better keep my voice down. I heard corn has ears.' If you're lucky enough to get a sponge for pudding, say 'You've got to be careful what you say about sponge. It absorbs everything.' Or you could pick your favourite joke so far. Good luck, and remember to make a note of how you got on.

How much did the dinner lady laugh?

☐ So much that custard came out of her nose.

☐ Just a trifle.

☐ You got told to stop holding up the queue.

☐ She told you that you'd better start bringing in a packed lunch from now on.

3rd September

Doctor, doctor! I feel ill.

Well, well, well.

No. III, ill, ill.

4th September

Where do cows, pigs and sheep go to get cough medicine?

To a farm-acy.

OINKMENT

PORCINE
PRESCRIPTIONS
ONLY

IF YOU
FEEL UNWELL
ASK FOR A
HAMBULANCE

DAINTY
PIGGY
TROT

5th September

My dog is a cross between a cocker spaniel and a poodle. It's cute but it wakes me up really early every morning with a big smelly number two.

Yes, I'm always getting woken by a cocker-poodle poo.

6th September

Why should you never employ teachers to work in shops?

They'll take the register.

7th September

In 1533 on this day, Queen Elizabeth the First was born. She knighted Sir Francis Drake, which was odd considering he was both a pirate and a duck. Quack-*arrrs*! Liz only bathed once a year, which must have been how she *stank* the Spanish Armada. The Armada was a fleet of ships named after the popular cry of its sailors, 'Ah'm-'arder than you.' Please don't include any of these facts in your schoolwork, as they are made up. If you wanted a history book you should have bought one. Here's your joke.

What did the queen say as she rested the sword on the footballer's shoulder?
Man, you knighted!

8th September

My wife worked in a zoo when I met her.
I thought to myself, she's definitely a keeper.

9th September

I just wrote a whole book without any punctuation.

It was totally pointless.

Joke Challenge: Grammar Time

If you think learning punctuation is pointless, then you're definitely doing it wrong. I'm sure you'll soon *comma* to your senses, so don't *dash* off just yet. Your challenge is to write down as many words about language as you can and come up with your own joke. Colons, dashes, full stops, clauses and sentences – all of these terms have different meanings. So it might be something like: why was the criminal so happy when the judge said 'Send him down'? Because it was such a short sentence. Or can you work out what's wrong with this sentence: *'Santa is Father Christmas and Father Christmas is Santa, but Father Christmas is Santa.'* That's right. There are too many clauses.

Now it's your turn.
Write your grammar gag here:

....

....

....

....

....

10th September

I've got this lollipop lady who makes me so angry.

She really gets me a-cross.

11th September

Most of my jobs went smoothly, but my job repairing the rollercoaster had its ups and downs.

12th September

What do you call a woman who's good with books?

Library Anne.

13th September

Why didn't dinosaurs laugh?

They were pre-hysteric animals.

14th September

In my experience, people with drills and pickaxes are so selfish.
Because it's always mine, mine, mine.

15th September

On this day in 1890 Agatha Christie was born. She wrote over eighty murder-mystery stories. That's quite some body of work – a body found in the library, of course. She created the character of Hercule Poirot, a Belgian detective with elegant facial hair, who was always in a hurry to get his villain – he was very proud of his *must-dash*. She also created a sweet old lady detective, Miss Marple. Agatha Christie was once at the centre of a mystery in real life when she went missing for a few days – leading some to believe she had lost her *Marples*. But her enduring popularity is no mystery so in honour of Agatha, here's a sleuth-y gag.

Did you hear about the case of the dog in the freezer?
Unfortunately the lead went cold.

16th September

What did the lion call the stampeding wildebeest?

Fast food.

Joke Challenge: Matter-of-Fact Jokes

Today's joke has an element of truth. Wildebeest can run eighty kilometres per hour. Unfortunately for the wildebeest, so can lions – so the joke is pretty accurate, apart from the fact that obviously lions don't really talk. This week's challenge is to see if you can make a joke out of a fact. Maybe you've learned something at school or just read one in a book. Something like: 'We learned about gravity today . . . It was a bit of a downer.' Or 'I learned about adjectival phrases today. Very boring.'

Write your fact joke here:

. . . .

. . . .

. . . .

17th September

That new fart-fuelled car didn't get far.
No, it ran out of gas.

18th September

When it's hot my teacher makes us stand around flapping our arms to keep her cool. I don't like her much so I don't flap very hard.
I'm not her greatest fan.

19th September

Arr, Jim lad, I be talking like a farmer who's drunk too much rum. That can only mean one thing.
It must be **Talk Like a Pirate Day**. Hoist the main sail! Raise the anchor and haul in jokes with *arrrr!* in the punchline.

What's a group of thieving seafaring fighters called?
A pirate *arrrr*my!

What's the difference between Pilates and pirates?

The *arrrr*.

Why are there so many pirate jokes?

There just *arrrr*!

And now, here's today's pirate joke.

What do you call a snotty-nosed pirate in charge of punishments?

The planker-chief.

This cold will be the death of me.

20th September

Two lions are waiting to board Noah's ark. One says: 'Why does Noah get to take his whole family, but we animals are only allowed on in twos?' The other lion says: 'The guy's got double standards . . .'

21st September

My cat acts like it works for the police. **It's a real cop-y cat.**

22nd September

How do you know if a cartoon is unwell? **He looks drawn.**

> **I don't get it!** If you say somebody looks 'drawn' it means they look very tired.

Joke Challenge:
Cartoon Time

This book is full of fabulous illustrations by the legendary Nigel Parkinson, who knows a bit about funny cartoons. This week's challenge is to draw something funny. If you're not sure what to start with, pick a favourite joke from this book and turn it into a cartoon. Happy doodling.

Draw your doodle here:

23rd September

Why did the guitarist pluck both guitars?
He simply couldn't pick one.

> **I don't get it!** 'Picking' a guitar is when you play the strings individually and not all together at once, which would be strumming.

24th September

Today we celebrate Pigs in Space, neurotic frogs, the word 'Mahna Mahna' and small blue creatures being shot out of cannons. Happy birthday to **Jim Henson,** creator of the Muppets. Kermit and the gang have been going strong since the 1970s and they're still making people laugh today. Weirdly, they haven't aged at all. Our favourite is Fozzie Bear, a stand-up comedian with some truly terrible jokes. I wonder why that is. Here's today's groaner.

Where does Miss Piggy keep her lipstick?
In a ham-bag.

25th September

When do cars stop running?
When they're exhausted.

26th September

What's the best way to steal Cleopatra's lunch?
Seize her salad.

> **I don't get it!** 'Seize her' sounds like Caesar, the Roman emperor, who was in love with Cleopatra. There is also a famous salad called a Caesar Salad, and although it has nothing to do with the Roman emperor, lettuce go with it!

27th September

Whenever we were naughty, our dad would make us wear a shell and eat nothing but lettuce.
That taught-us.

28th September

Apparently Donald Trump once stole someone's ice cream.

Of course, he says it's just flake news.

29th September

Why was the welder feeling so gloomy?
He lost his spark.

30th September

In the court case about gravity, everyone got sent down. Well, everyone except the guy with the jetpack, who got given a suspended sentence.
He was so happy, his feet didn't touch the ground.

OCTOBER

October was named after the creation of experimental scientist Professor Mick Summup, who specialised in mixing up animals together. He tried to mix a pelican with an eel and a giraffe, but the electricity bills were too high. He tried mixing a snake, a fish and a skunk. The result was 'armless enough but a bit smelly. October took its name from the weirdest combination of all. Those who saw the result say it had eight tentacles with razor-sharp claws at the end. It would scare off any attackers with a growl and by leaking ink. Half octopus, half bear, it was the ferocious . . . OCTO-BEAR! Happy October, everyone!

1st October

It's **International Day of Older Persons**. Old people aren't what they used to be. In my day, they used to show respect to children. Also, these days, old people are all online. I think they mostly use 'old Facebook'. Talking of which, here's a good old joke:

Ever looked at old people and wondered if they were vampires?

Perhaps it's because they're long in the tooth.

Joke Challenge:
Golden Oldies

You've had to ask other people for jokes in previous challenges, but for this week's challenge it needs to be someone at least two generations older than you. Old people can be a great source of funny material - and we're not talking about your grandma's curtains. And make sure you offer one of your jokes in return.

Write your older person's joke here:

....

....

....

....

2nd October

Oh no! The river's run dry! We're all going to die from thirst!

Come on, that's just a little ex-stream.

3rd October

How do you spy on a computer?
Keep tabs on it.

4th October

Did you hear about the porcupine that got stuck in a freezer?
It was spine-chilling.

5th October

It's **World Teachers' Day**, which means it's time to MAKE YOUR TEACHER LAUGH AGAIN. Teachers do a great job. It can't be easy being responsible for so many *rulers*. Some of them do find it hard to get their pupils under control – that must be why so many have to wear glasses. There are lots of teacher jokes out there, but give this one a go.

How did the fronted adverbial arrive at the party?
Suddenly, he arrived at the party.

You do have to get the words spot on for that one. Here's another joke designed to amuse your teacher:

Why did the school inspector challenge the teacher to a blinking competition?
It was an off-stared inspection.

6th October

I auditioned to play the part of an old baker.
They said I was too young for the *roll*. I'm not *sourdough*.

7th October

How did the first two pigs feel after a visit from the wolf?
Totally blown away.

8th October

Why did the widower only grieve in the afternoon?
He wasn't really a mourning person.

Joke Challenge:
The Dark Side

'Dark humour' is a term used to refer to jokes that deal with the more serious side of life . . . and, well, death. It can be a sensitive area, but that doesn't mean you should necessarily shy away from it. For example:

Did you hear the joke about the zombie clown?

It was dead funny.

Or:

Did you hear about the herb villain?
He killed thyme.

Or even:

How did the dead celebrity manage to write a book?
He used a ghostwriter.

Now see if you can come up with one.

Comedy Tip All comedy involves knowing your audience. Some of these jokes will make your friends laugh. Some of them are more suitable for your parents so pick wisely.

9th October

It's **World Post Day,** which is a first-class reason for a post joke. We could have gone for the one about how ants never go in post offices – they fear the stamp. We could have picked the one about how postal workers always have such good handwriting – they take pride in the lettering. In the end we went with:

Why do rabbits like post offices?
They just like the lettuce.

10th October

Why should you be nice to volcanoes?
Because they're lava-ly.

11th October

What do you call a yoga teacher who works too much?
Overstretched.

12th October

I've got a job milking famous cows.
It's on a legend-dairy farm.

13th October

On the second Friday of October, we celebrate all things eggy because it's **World Egg Day**. Not all egg jokes are bad. Some are *yolk-ay*. Some are just *all-white*. While the reason the chicken crossed the road will remain forever a mystery, I can answer the question of which came first, the chicken or the egg? Obviously, it was the egg . . . a dinosaur egg.

Did you hear about the shy chick?
It took him ages to come out of his shell.

14th October

What do pandas shout to make you jump?
Bam–BOO!

15th October

My career in sewage went down the drain.
My job emptying bins was a load of rubbish.
So I got a job as a road sweeper, and totally cleaned up.

Joke Challenge: Funny Job

Whether or not you know what you want to be when you grow up, you can have a lot of fun with job jokes. For example, when you worked as a scarecrow you were considered *outstanding in your field*. Perhaps you used to work in a pit stop, pumping up tyres but in the end you *couldn't deal with the pressure*. Or maybe you found your job as a police officer *too arresting*.

Write your job joke here:

....

....

....

....

16th October

How do birds learn how to fly?
They just wing it.

17th October

Why can't miners eat cabbage?
I don't know, it's just coals law.

18th October

What do you call someone whose job is wiping the bottoms of rich people?
A butt-ler.

19th October

Have you seen those packets of magic singing biscuits?
They contain four tune cookies.

20th October

What do mathematicians do
when hungry?
**They crunch the numbers
and make a pie chart.**

21st October

There's a new cookery show about
pork products.
It's called The Great British Bacon.

22nd October

I recently got crushed by a pile of books.
**I suppose I've only got my shelf
to blame.**

Joke Challenge:
One for the Books

There are lots of book jokes in this joke book. That's because it's been written by a couple of people who spend their time writing books. Perhaps you've read one of them. If not, the authors of this book heartily recommend you do so at once. Which brings us on to this week's challenge. Recommend a funny book to a friend then ask for a recommendation in return.

Then read it.

Then laugh.

End of story.

23rd October

How did Mrs Dracula know that Mr Dracula was ill?

The coffin.

24th October

Why aren't athletes trained by sloths?
They're slow coaches.

25th October

It's Pablo Picasso's birthday. Some of his paintings are such good listeners. Seriously, they're all ears. Mind you - good painter, terrible driver. His eyes were all over the place. In honour of the great cubist, here's today's joke.

I like the idea of doing a self-portrait.
It's something I can really see myself doing.

26th October

Where do aliens and extra-terrestrials go when they hurt themselves?
A & ET.

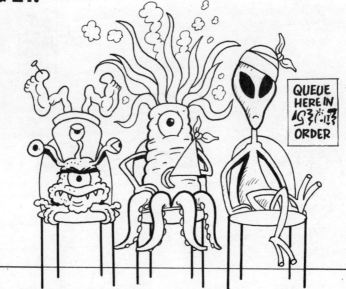

27th October

Captain James Cook was born on this day in 1728. He became a celebrity after travelling to what is now Australia and New Zealand. He met a sticky ending, though, when he was killed and his body parts were boiled – not because his captors were cannibals, but possibly because they thought his name was an instruction.

How do we know that Captain Cook played hide-and-seek?

Because he lost his hide while seeking Australia.

28th October

When do mountaineers retire?

When they reach the peak of their careers.

29th October

How many famous vampires can you mention?

One if you count Dracula.

30th October

What do you do if you discover that fifty zombies are approaching your house?

Hope it's Halloween!

31st October

Happy Halloween! Grab your broomsticks, gnash your teeth and wave your wands in the air like you just don't care. That's the spirit. Remember, on Halloween, things that go *pumpkin the night* are good. You should have plenty of spooky jokes now to extract a giggle from even the deadest zombie in the graveyard. Here's one more.

When are you safe from a zombie?

When they're past their chews-by date.

Joke Challenge: **Trick or Treat . . . or Laugh.**

This year, instead of saying, 'Trick or treat' cry 'Titter or treat!', then earn your sweets by telling a spooky joke. Maybe you'll be so funny you'll get an extra handful of sweets. Or maybe your jokes will die and you'll get a door in the face. Use one of ours – or, even better, make up your own. It could be about ghosts, ghouls, vampires, witches or werewolves.

How did it go down?

☐ Spook-tastic! Everyone loved my gags.

☐ Er, pretty well, although there was a lot of groaning.

☐ My jokes scared everyone off.

☐ They took sweets off me after hearing my jokes.

NOVEMBER

Remember, remember . . . something. I forget what. Oh yes, Fireworks Night. Don't forget to lock up your pets before you go shooting fireworks into the sky. And whatever you do, don't get mixed up and lock up your fireworks before you shoot your pets in the sky. We made that mistake once, thinking the hamster wheel was a Catherine wheel. We never did find out where Mr Fluffy landed. Probably *Hamster-dam*. Although, after coming down that fast, he'd probably be more like *hamster-jam*! We're joking, of course. We have never accidentally fired a hamster into the sky and no one can prove otherwise.

1st November

The sloth in my class is so behind. The frog in my class has come on leaps and bounds.

But the giraffe in my class is the real *high achiever*.

2nd November

What do you call a well-rounded knight?
Sir Cumference.

3rd November

I went for a curry with James Bond,
Dangermouse and Alex Rider last night.
It was all right, but a bit too spies-y.

4th November

What do you need when consuming hot beverages in the car?

A safe-tea belt.

Joke challenge: Let's Split!

In today's joke, we've taken the word SAFETY and split it up to make SAFE-TEA. So this week's challenge is to find a word and see whether you can pull it apart and make it into a joke. We went for a word ending in -ty (tea), but there are also heaps of words that sound like 'tree' at the end. So chemistry could become 'chemist tree' and you could make a joke about where medicine grows. Or Sherlock Holmes' favourite word 'elementary' could become 'a lemon tree' and you could make a joke about how he solved the mystery of the fruit.

Write your joke here:

. . . .

. . . .

. . . .

. . . .

. . . .

5th November

It's **Fireworks Night** – a night where we light up Guy Fawkes, who tried and failed to blow up Parliament on this day in 1605. I suppose it must have had a puncture. Guy's plan *blew up* in his face – which is more than can be said for his collection of gunpowder barrels. BOOM BOOM!

Why don't we shoot water into the air on 5th November?

Because fire works better.

6th November

Why don't fish use Google?
**Because they don't like being online
. . . or have anything to with the net.**

7th November

Knock knock!
Who's there?
Twitter.
Twitter who?
Oh, there's an owl at the door.

8th November

What do cavemen like best about school?
The after-school CLUBS!

9th November

What music do bunnies like?
Hop-hop.

10th November

I've got plans to build a wall. Nothing's set in stone yet, though.

11th November

Joke Challenge:
Picture This

There's something odd about today's joke. Have you spotted what it is? That's right. There are no words. That's because you have to work a little harder than usual. Your challenge is to look at today's picture and come up with your own joke about what's happening. Maybe you've done this with some of the other pictures in the book, but it's a fun way of coming up with jokes that are original to you. So, have fun and make it funny.

Write your joke here:

. . . .

. . . .

. . . .

. . . .

. . . .

. . . .

. . . .

. . . .

. . . .

12th November

I've got this new feature on my phone that tells me when I should have a little sleep.
You know, an app.

13th November

Today we are celebrating **World Kindness Day**, which is our kind of day. It's nice to be nice but it's also good to be funny – so long as your jokes are not mean. You should always be cautious about jokes that involve stereotypes of gender, religion or nationality. But with these two, you're on safe ground.

Why are German children the nicest in the world?
Because they're kinder.

What did the Spanish fireman name his children?
Hose A and Hose B.

> **I don't get it!** The first joke uses the double meaning of the word **kinder**: in German it means 'children'; in English it means being more kind. The second plays with the pronunciation of the common Spanish name 'José' sounding like Hose A.

14th November

What's the worst thing about learning to sing?
All the hum work.

15th November

Why did the wizard bring a dragon to school?

It was his school blazer.

16th November

Why did the archaeologist retire?
His life was in ruins.

17th November

Did you hear about the boxer who retired to play video games?

He's an ex-boxer now.

18th November

Why aren't footballers allowed to work in mail-rooms?

From time to time they've been known to hit the post.

Joke Challenge:
Address Your Fans

When do you get anything exciting through the post? Just on your birthday, right? Or maybe you have a subscription to a comic. This week's challenge is to write and post a letter. And no, we don't mean pop the letter 'A' through the letterbox. Send a few well-chosen jokes to a friend or a relative you don't see very often. They'll be excited to open the envelope, and then they'll be totally tickled to read your funny-mail inside. You could include a daft drawing too if you like. And, once you've written your letter, why not put something hilarious on the envelope to make the postal worker laugh, too?

Tell us who you wrote your letter to:

. . . .

. . . .

. . . .

. . . .

19th November

It's **World Toilet Day**, which highlights the importance of fresh water and sanitation. But it also gives us an excuse to squeeze out a couple of toilet jokes. Whether they float or sink, I only hope you don't think they stink.

Toilet joke number one is:

Why did the toilet look clean?
It had a wee wash.

And here's number two:

Did you hear about the famous poo?
It was just a flush in the pan.

20th November

Did you hear about the palaeontologist who lifted a T-rex?

He used dino-might.

21st November

It's **World Television Day.** In 1925 (so just before half past seven) John Logie Baird demonstrated the first ever television in a famous London shop called Selfridges. This was a bit stupid because Baird was trying to sell a television, not a fridge. Unfortunately, no one had thought to invent television programmes yet so it took a long time for his invention to catch on. Some older people call it 'the box' because televisions used to look like boxes. These days they look more like trays, which makes sense because there really is a lot on them. Some of it is even funny. And now, later than advertised, here's your joke.

How do you make a TV giggle?
Tickle its telly button.

22nd November

How do you know if a field is friendly?
Because of the long wavy grass.

23rd November

It's **Dr Who Day**! If you don't know your Silence
from your Cybermen from your Daleks, then
you're not going to enjoy this timely joke. In fact,
you probably won't get any of it – I'm *Galli-fraid*
not, because our favourite time-travelling series

comes with all sorts of jargon. TARDIS, sonic screwdriver, wibbly-wobbly-timey-wimey . . . It's a whole other dimension. So sit tight as we go back in time and then forward again to bring you a joke from back there in the future. We just regenerated it.

What do you get if two Time Lords turn up in the same *Dr Who* episode?
A pair o' docs.

> **I don't get it!** A pair o' docs sounds like **a paradox**. So you get a pair of doctors but you also end up with something that doesn't make sense, which is called a paradox. Dr Who loves to solve paradoxes!

24th November

Did you hear about the magical head louse?
It played Quidd-itch.

25th November

Did you hear about the man who committed some heavyweight crimes?

He was a shoplifter.

26th November

How does a baby learn new things on the internet?
It gurgles it.

27th November

Why were the butcher's arms so long?
Because the steaks were so high.

28th November

Do vegetarians object to Sunday lunches?
No, they don't have beef with it.

29th November

Did you know there's a new website for vampires?

Vlog the Impaler.

30th November

Why didn't the poltergeist sit on the sofa?

Because it was in the living room.

DECEMBER

It's that time of the year again when everyone starts going *Christmas crackers*! Joke-wise, December is festively full of funnies. Is it *Santa Claus* . . . or a *Santa Clause* . . . or even *Santa Claws*? Do elves work for the *National Elf Service* or are they *'elf-employed*? What happens if they lack *'elf-discipline*? Does Santa give them the *sack*? The weather might be bad, but does it look like *rain, dear,* or is that a *reindeer*? Yes, there are stacks of Christmas jokes so start *stocking up* now. And when you write your Christmas list, be sure to include a joke to get Santa going ho-ho-ho!

1st December

How do you clean a Christmas tree?
Give it a bauble bath.

2nd December

What's the best way to start creating a new galaxy?
Planet!

Joke Challenge: **Write a Spaced-Out Joke!**

We love space. *Or-bits* of it at least. If you ever get a chance to go through an airlock you should see it as a real opportunity; one door closes and another one opens. That's what they say. And have you heard this story about the moon's orbit? It's been *going around* for a while. Experts will tell you that the universe is still expanding. Why? I suppose it wants more *space*.

Now it's your turn. Write down all of the space words you can think of then get to work on your joke. We all know what you do if you see a space man. Park in it, man.

Your best space joke:

. . . .

. . . .

. . . .

. . . .

. . . .

3rd December

I just sewed the holes up in your jeans.
It made me really angry.
My fault, really. I used cross-stitch.

4th December

How do you turn a dog into a doctor?
Make it heel.

5th December

I gave up reading the crystal ball.
I couldn't see a future in it.

6th December

A pirate just told me that my last girlfriend is sitting on a load of treasure.
He said, ex marks the spot.

7th December

Teacher: Why were you running in the school corridor?
Pupil: How else do you exercise books?

8th December

Teacher: Why have you brought your phones into class?
Pupils: You told us to come in with our texts!

9th December

Did you hear about the comedian who performed at a tea party?

He stirred up a right brew-ha-ha.

> **I don't get it!** A 'brouhaha' is a fuss. As it's made up of the words 'brew' and 'ha-ha' it's perfect for comedy tea joke.

Joke Challenge:
Cause to Celebrate

December is the party month and parties are a great opportunity to find new audiences for your jokes. Whether it's a birthday party, a street party, a tea party, a family get-together or a spontaneous shindig, it's a great opportunity to eat, drink and be silly. And now you're a seasoned joker, you should have no problem breaking the ice. And no, we don't mean marching around your little sister's party, crushing ice. (No one likes a party-crusher.) The next time you're at a party, make sure you have a few cracking jokes, then go around cracking them.

How did your jokes go down at the party?

☐ Amazing. I was crowned Party King.

☐ Not bad. A few people even laughed.

☐ I got a couple of smiles but no belly laughs.

☐ I've got a lifelong party ban. Thanks a bunch.

10th December

How do flower fairies fight?
With blades of grass.

11th December

We did subtraction today in maths.
I'll be honest, I took nothing away from it.

12th December

Our school has started combining subjects. Yesterday I did maths combined with woodwork.

We made a times table.

13th December

I'm in the school football team.

What position do you play?

Like this, mostly.

14th December

How do you order duck feathers on the internet?
Down-load them.

> **I don't get it!** 'Down' is the word for the light, fluffy protective covering that ducks have under their feathers to keep them warm.

15th December

It's **International Tea Day**. Would you be-*leaf* it – this beverage gets to *bag*sy a whole day to itself. Tea gets drunk all over the world and there are around 1,500 types of tea. There is the kind you drink when you want to tell the truth (*honest-tea*). There is one for drinking on your own (*individuali-tea*). Lots of people drink it to give them more *respectabili-tea* or *credibili-tea*. And then there is the kind favoured by astronomers – *infini-tea*.

Why are teabags troublesome?
Because they're always getting into hot water.

16th December

What did the flower say to the unwanted plant on the lawn?
Hey, you weed on the grass.

Joke Challenge:
Poo-tiful Jokes

We talked about toilet humour in April, but when it comes to toilet matters, it's no bad thing to be *regular*. That's the *bottom* line. It *wee*-ly is. Psychologists say that toilet humour is an important part of a child's development – which is definitely worth using as an excuse because this week's challenge is to write your own original toilet joke. Take a word associated with toilets (loo, bog, potty, nappy, wee, poo, poop, fart, bum, bottom) then see if you can turn it into a joke.

What's brown and sits on a desk?
A com-pooter.

What poo is it OK to put on your head?
Sham-poo.

What curry can you eat in the toilet?
A vinda-loo.

Now, it's your turn.

Write your toilet joke here:

....

....

....

....

....

Comedy Tip Once again, remember to pick your audience.
Not everyone will appreciate your toilet humour.

17th December

I think my brother and sister must be clockwork.
Why?
Because Dad says they keep winding each other up.

18th December

What do you say when offering a sweet to a Pokémon?
Pick-a-chew.

19th December

How do gorillas study for their exams?
They knuckle down.

20th December

Did you hear about the new TV show about salads in the jungle?

I'M A CELERY, GET ME OUT OF HERE!

21st December

Teacher: Billy, why have you brought a kangaroo in a Santa hat to school?

Billy: You said it was Christmas jumper day.

22nd December

Why was the Hanukkah Monster called the Hanukkah Monster?

Because it eight candles.

> **I don't get it!** Hanukkah is a Jewish celebration that takes place over eight nights. On each of those nights, a candle is lit. As far as we know, there is no Hanukkah monster that eats the candles.

23rd December

What goes 'oh oh oh'?

Father Christmas walking backwards.

Joke Challenge:
It's a Cracker!

For a joker, this is the best present ever – a joke so bad you don't know if you should laugh or cry (you've probably seen some good examples in this book!). Remember to collect the one-liners and big groaners that fall out of your Christmas crackers. Perhaps they're not even the tiniest bit funny, but don't give up! Try delivering them in different ways to see if you can make them better. You've had plenty of practice by now. See how many family members you can make laugh with your cracker joke, and then make up a ticklingly terrible cracker-style joke of your own and tell it. Did your family guess it was yours?

Your cracker joke:

. . . .

. . . .

. . . .

. . . .

. . . .

. . . .

How many real cracker jokes
got a laugh?...

What was the worst (therefore best)
cracker joke you found?

....
....
....

24th December

Why shouldn't you give your snowman
teeth?
Frostbite.

25th December

Happy Christmas, everyone! This is going to
be the best ever! Yes, Christmas presents are
always better than Christmas past! Hopefully
your stockings and pillowcases are stuffed
with goodies – and not your grandma's legs or
pillows. Lots of families play games at Christmas.

Charades we find *unspeakably* dull. We never win Pictionary – we only ever *draw*. Twister is our favourite, though. We'll *bend over backwards* to play that. And then there's Christmas dinner. It's usually a real *turkey* of a meal . . . which is *nuts* for vegetarians.

But we like to liven it up by playing blow-football with my sprouts. You do have to be careful with sprout football, though: one can too easily blow off.

Why does Father Christmas give his helpers medical checks?

To see if they're elfy.

NATIONAL ELF SERVICE

26th December

It's Boxing Day but that is not an excuse for putting on a pair of padded gloves and pummelling your siblings. Boxing Day actually got its name from a tradition of giving boxes to servants. If we got given an empty box for Christmas, we'd flip our *lids*. Mind you, it's worth hanging on to those boxes in case you move house, although you do need a pretty big box to fit a whole house in. Here's your joke.

Knock knock!

Who's there?

Arthur.

Arthur who?

Arthur any mince pies left?

27th December

Where do toilets go to pray?
The cistern chapel!

> **I don't get it!** In the Vatican in Rome, where the Pope
> lives, there is a chapel with a fabulous ceiling painted by
> Michelangelo. It's called the Sistine Chapel. A cistern (which
> sounds very similar) is what holds all the loo water before you
> flush!

28th December

How do parts of the body connect?
Cell phones.

29th December

Doctor, doctor! My farts sound like
flutes and clarinets.
Hmm, sounds like woodwind.

30th December

How does Gandalf like his tea?
With the Baggins.

31st December

Adam: I'll be able to hear you so much better tomorrow.

Eve: Why?

Adam: God said today we'd be celebrating new 'ears, Eve. And tomorrow it's new 'ears day!

Joke Challenge:
Encore, Encore

So did you manage it? Did you read a joke a day? Be honest. Or were there a couple of months when this book ended up under your bed, covered in dust with nothing but an old odd sock for company? Don't worry, all is forgiven. And although this year is over, your mission to be funny will never end. Your challenge is to continue spreading joy and laughter for the rest of your life. And your challenge is to make next year YOUR FUNNIEST YEAR EVER!

Acknowledgements

Many thanks to my laughing stock – all those who helped inspire the jokes – and to Jerome, who is super funny, even if not always intentionally. And very special thanks to our funny girl, Allie Lefever. You rock!

Rachel

Thank you to all of my friends and family who laughed harder at the idea that I was writing a joke book than they ever did at my jokes.

Gareth

To find out more about Rachel and Gareth's other funny books, visit their websites:

www.racheldelahaye.com
and
www.garethwrites.co.uk

If this book has inspired you to come up with a brilliant joke, why not email it to the authors at TheDailyJoker@mail.com?

Piccadilly
PRESS

Thank you for choosing a Piccadilly Press book.

If you would like to know more about our authors, our books or if you'd just like to know what we're up to, you can find us online.

www.piccadillypress.co.uk

You can also find us on:

We hope to see you soon!